Early United States

HARCOURT BRACE SOCIAL STUDIES

ACTIVITY BOOK

Teacher's Edition

HARCOURT BRACE & COMPANY

Orlando Atlanta Austin Boston San Francisco Chicago Dallas

New York Toronto London

Visit The Learning Site at http://www.hbschool.com

For permission to reprint copyrighted material, grateful acknowledgment is made to the following sources:

Chelsea House Publishers, a division of Main Line Book Co.: From "If You Miss Me from the Back of the Bus" in *Songs of Protest and Civil Rights,* compiled by Jerry Silverman. Lyrics copyright © 1992 by Chelsea House Publishers, a division of Main Line Book Co.

Dutton Children's Books, a division of Penguin Putnam Inc.: From *Immigrant Kids* by Russell Freedman. Text copyright © 1980 by Russell Freedman.

The McGraw-Hill Companies: From book #60660 *The Log of Christopher Columbus* by Robert H. Fuson. Text copyright 1987 by Robert H. Fuson. Original English language edition published by International Marine Publishing Company, Camden, ME.

Printed in the United States of America

ISBN 0-15-310312-4

10 073 02

The activities in this book reinforce or extend social studies concepts and skills in **EARLY UNITED STATES.** There is one activity for each lesson and skill. Reproductions of the activity pages appear with answers in the Teacher's Edition.

Contents

UNIT 1

Chapter 1

Lesson 1	A Native American Belief	1
Skill	How to Compare Map Projections	2–3
Lesson 2	Think Like an Archaeologist	4
Skill	How to Identify Patterns on Time Lines	5
Lesson 3	Preserving Native American Artifacts	6
Chapter Review	The First Americans	7

Chapter 2

Lesson 1	Two Northwest Coast Indian Canoes	8
Lesson 2	Learning About Kachinas	9
Lesson 3	The Importance of the Buffalo	10
Lesson 4	Hiawatha & Longfellow Make History	11
Skill	How to Identify Causes and Effects	12
Lesson 5	Unlocking the Mystery of Mayan Numbers	13
Chapter Review	Indians of North America	14

UNIT 2

Chapter 3

Lesson 1	A Viking Ship	15
Lesson 2	Marco Polo and the Riches of Asia	16
Lesson 3	The Log of Christopher Columbus	17
Skill	How to Use Latitude and Longitude	18
Lesson 4	The Costs of Exploration	19
Skill	How to Form a Logical Conclusion	20
Chapter Review	The Age of Exploration	21

Chapter 4

Lesson 1	A Day in Tenochtitlán	22
Lesson 2	Estéban in Time and Place	23
Lesson 3	Do You Speak Spanish?	24
Skill	How to Use a Map to Show Movement	25

Lesson 4	Preparing Furs for Trade	26
Lesson 5	Harvest Festivals	27
Skill	How to Read Parallel Time Lines	28
Chapter Review	Encounters in the Americas	29

UNIT 3

Chapter 5

Lesson 1	Comparing Spanish Missions	30
Lesson 2	A Taste of Louisiana	31
Lesson 3	The Routes of Three Colonists	32
Lesson 4	The Middle Colonies	33
Lesson 5	Comparing the Colonies	34–35
Skill	How to Classify Information	36
Chapter Review	Europeans Settle Throughout North America	37

Chapter 6

Lesson 1	Having a Whale of a Time	38
Skill	How to Read a Circle Graph	39
Lesson 2	Looking at Life in the Southern Colonies	40
Lesson 3	Tooling Around the Frontier	41
Skill	How to Use a Product Map to Make Generalizations	42
Chapter Review	Life in the British Colonies	43

UNIT 4

Chapter 7

Lesson 1	Historical Events of the 1700s	44
Skill	How to Use a Historical Map	45
Lesson 2	Understanding Proverbs in *Poor Richard's Almanack*	46
Lesson 3	Events Leading to Revolution	47
Skill	How to Make Economic Choices	48
Chapter Review	Differences Divide Britain and Its Colonies	49

Chapter 8

Lesson 1	The Redcoats Are Coming!	50
Skill	How to Read a Political Cartoon	51
Lesson 2	A Woman Printed the Declaration of Independence	52
Skill	How to Learn from Pictures	53

Lesson 3	Americans Take Sides	54
Lesson 4	Characterize Patriots	55
Lesson 5	Which Event Happened First?	56
Chapter Review	The War for Independence	57

UNIT 5

Chapter 9

Lesson 1	Articles of Confederation	58
Lesson 2	Who Was There?	59
Skill	How to Figure Travel Time and Distance	60
Lesson 3	Who Has the Power?	61
Skill	How to Compromise to Resolve Conflicts	62
Lesson 4	Who Does What in the Government?	63
Lesson 5	Constitutional Footnotes	64
Chapter Review	The Constitution	65

Chapter 10

Lesson 1	The Maze of Ratification	66
Lesson 2	Counting the Amendments	67
Lesson 3	Who's in Office?	68
Skill	How to Learn from a Document	69
Chapter Review	A New Government Begins	70

UNIT 6

Chapter 11

Lesson 1	Blazing a Trail West	71
Lesson 2	Follow Their Footsteps	72
Lesson 3	The Growth of Nationalism	73
Skill	How to Predict a Likely Outcome	74
Lesson 4	The Flag Was Still There	75
Chapter Review	On the Move	76

Chapter 12

Lesson 1	Inventors and Their Inventions	77
Lesson 2	The Trail of Tears	78
Lesson 3	The Oregon Trail	79
Skill	How to Use Relief and Elevation Maps	80
Lesson 4	Seneca Falls	81
Skill	How to Use a Double-Bar Graph	82–83
Chapter Review	The Way West	84

UNIT 7

Chapter 13

Lesson 1	A Tale of Two Regions, 1860	85
Skill	How to Use Graphs to Identify Trends	86
Lesson 2	The Life and Times of a Slave	87
Lesson 3	"Bleeding Kansas"	88
Lesson 4	Why Did South Carolina Secede?	89
Skill	How to Make a Thoughtful Decision	90
Chapter Review	Background to the Conflict	91

Chapter 14

Lesson 1	The Bonnie Blue Flag	92
Lesson 2	The Emancipation Proclamation	93
Lesson 3	Civil War Horses	94
Skill	How to Compare Maps with Different Scales	95
Lesson 4	It's in the Bag!	96
Chapter Review	Civil War and Reconstruction	97

UNIT 8

Chapter 15

Lesson 1	Famous Entrepreneurs	98
Skill	How to Use a Time Zone Map	99–100
Lesson 2	Duke Ellington	101
Lesson 3	Organizing Resources	102
Lesson 4	School Days	103
Skill	How to Solve a Problem	104
Chapter Review	A Changing America	105

Chapter 16

Lesson 1	Immigration	106
Skill	How to Compare Information on Graphs	107
Lesson 2	An African American Portrait	108
Lesson 3	Sing About Civil Rights	109
Skill	How to Act as a Responsible Citizen	110
Lesson 4	An American Song	111
Chapter Review	The Promise of America	112

A Native American Belief

Understand Oral History

DIRECTIONS: Read the following quotation. It describes what some Native Americans believe about their origins and their rights. Then answer the questions that follow.

"When we were created we were given our ground to live on and from this time these were our rights. This is all true. We were put here by the Creator— I was not brought from a foreign country and did not come here. I was put here by the Creator."

—Chief Weninock, Yakima, 1915

1. According to this quotation, where did the first Americans come from?

from the Creator who put them on the land

2. Which sentence in the passage disagrees with the theory that the first Americans came across the Bering Strait? "We were put here by the Creator—I was not brought from a foreign country and did not come here."

3. In the passage, what does "these were our rights" refer to? the rights the Creator gave them to live on their ground

4. What can you conclude about Native Americans' beliefs about land rights?

Native Americans believe the land belongs to them because they were put on it by the Creator.

5. Why do you think Chief Weninock felt that he needed to state "This is all true"?

Responses should include reference to the scientific theories that deny the presence of native peoples in the Americas before migration.

HOW TO COMPARE MAP Projections

Only a globe can show exact shape, size, direction, and distance on the Earth. Cartographers try to show these four features of the Earth on a flat map as exactly as possible, but all map projections have distortions.

Apply Map and Globe Skills

DIRECTIONS: Study the map projections on this page and the following page. Then read each statement on the next page. Decide whether the statement applies to a Mercator projection, to a Mollweide projection, or to both projections. Place a check on the correct line or lines.

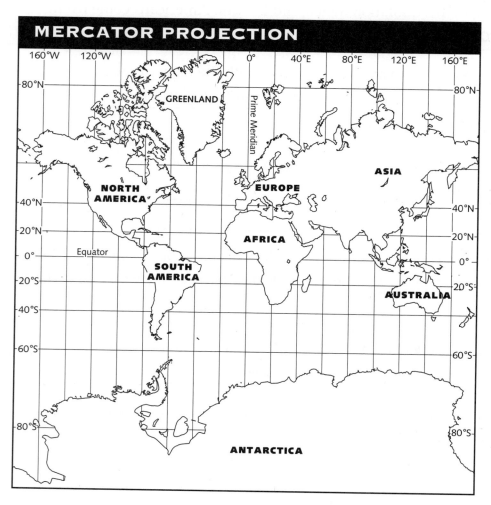

(continued)

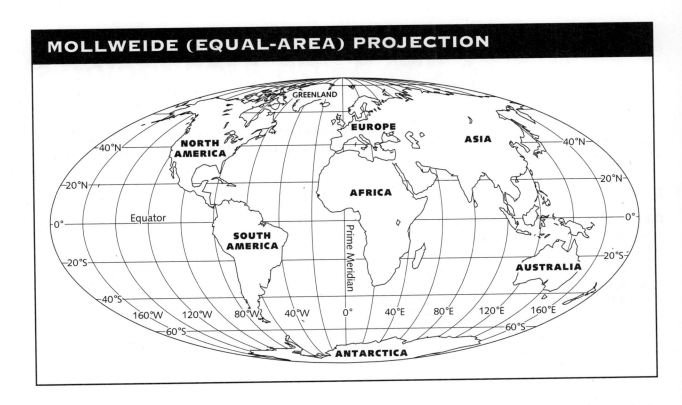

MOLLWEIDE (EQUAL-AREA) PROJECTION

Mercator **Mollweide**

Mercator	Mollweide	
✓	✓	**1.** Shows the seven continents.
	✓	**2.** Shows the curved feature of the Earth.
✓		**3.** Uses straight lines for all lines of latitude and longitude.
✓		**4.** Shows all lines of latitude and longitude at right angles to each other.
✓	✓	**5.** Uses a straight line for the equator.
✓	✓	**6.** Uses a straight line for the prime meridian.
	✓	**7.** Shows meridians intersecting at the top and bottom of the map.
✓	✓	**8.** Shows parallels NOT intersecting.
✓	✓	**9.** Uses straight lines to show latitude.
	✓	**10.** Shows sizes of places true to scale.
✓		**11.** Shows Greenland as about the same size as Africa.
	✓	**12.** Uses curved lines to show longitude.

Use after reading Chapter 1, Skill Lesson, pages 56–57.

THINK LIKE an Archaeologist

An archaeologist uses artifacts to learn about past cultures. Archaeologists are trained to find clues from artifacts in order to learn about a culture. They are also trained to know what clues artifacts do NOT give.

Interpret Visuals

DIRECTIONS: Study the following artifacts. Then write the name of the artifact that best answers the questions below.

Club
Made from wood.
Used for hunting.

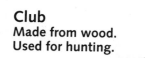

Bone Needle
Made from an animal bone splinter. Used to sew hides into clothing and tents.

Basket
Woven in different ways for different purposes. Used for gathering, preparing, and storing food.

Pottery
Made by coiling thin rolls of clay on top of one another. Used for storage and cooking.

Atlatl
Spear-throwing weapon made of wood.
Used for hunting.

1. Which artifact would have been the best to use to hunt the woolly mammoth?
atlatl

2. Which artifact shows that Native Americans made clothing? bone needle

3. Which two artifacts show that the Native Americans were food gatherers and farmers?
basket, pottery

4. Which three artifacts show that the Native Americans worked with crafts?
bone needle, basket, pottery

5. Which two artifacts could have been used for cooking? basket, pottery

Use after reading Chapter 1, Lesson 2, pages 58–63.

Harcourt Brace School Publishers

HOW TO IDENTIFY Patterns on Time Lines

Apply Chart and Graph Skills

DIRECTIONS: Each of the six statements that follow tells how many years ago an event occurred. For each one, change the number of years shown to a calendar date using B.C. To change, or convert, from number of years ago to a B.C. date, subtract 2,000. Write these dates in the spaces provided. Then write the question number of each event above the correct date on the time line.

1. The land bridge theory says the first people arrived in the Americas about

12,000 years ago. $\underline{\quad 12{,}000 - 2{,}000 = 10{,}000 \qquad 10{,}000 \text{ B.C.}\quad}$

2. Artifacts from about 13,000 years ago have been found in Monte Verde, Chile.

$\underline{\quad 13{,}000 - 2{,}000 = 11{,}000 \qquad 11{,}000 \text{ B.C.}\quad}$

3. Clovis points were first made about 11,600 years ago.

$\underline{\quad 11{,}600 - 2{,}000 = 9{,}600 \qquad 9600 \text{ B.C.}\quad}$

4. Giant mammals became extinct in the Americas about 10,000 years ago.

$\underline{\quad 10{,}000 - 2{,}000 = 8{,}000 \qquad 8000 \text{ B.C.}\quad}$

5. The last Ice Age ended about 10,000 years ago.

$\underline{\quad 10{,}000 - 2{,}000 = 8{,}000 \qquad 8000 \text{ B.C.}\quad}$

6. Farming was practiced in central Mexico 7,000 years ago.

$\underline{\quad 7{,}000 - 2{,}000 = 5{,}000 \qquad 5000 \text{ B.C.}\quad}$

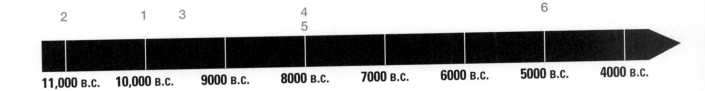

Harcourt Brace School Publishers

Use after reading Chapter 1, Skill Lesson, pages 64–65.

Preserving Native American Artifacts

Read Information in a Table

DIRECTIONS: The following table lists some of the best-preserved sites of early Native American settlements in North America. Use the information in the table to answer the questions that follow.

SITES OF NATIVE AMERICAN ARTIFACTS			
NAME OF SITE	**LOCATION**	**SIZE**	**FAST FACTS**
Chaco Canyon National Historical Park	Bloomfield, New Mexico	33 sq miles (85 sq km)	Contains 18 major ruins dating from about A.D. 920 to A.D. 1130. Pueblo Bonito (meaning "beautiful town") was one of the largest Native American apartment-style houses. It was about 5 stories high, had 800 rooms and 32 circular kivas, and housed more than 1,200 people.
Effigy Mounds National Monument	Near Marquette, Iowa	2 sq miles (5 sq km)	Has burial mounds shaped like birds and animals. The Mound Builder people were active from about 1000 B.C. to about A.D. 1500.
Mesa Verde National Park	Southwestern Colorado	53,036 acres	Occupied from about A.D. 1 to about A.D. 1300. One pueblo, the Cliff Palace, held up to 1,000 people and had 200 rooms. Abandoned about two centuries before Europeans arrived in the Americas.
Petrified Forest National Park	Near Holbrook, Arizona	93,493 acres	Occupied A.D. 500 and remained occupied for 1,000 years. Preserves Native American petroglyphs (rock carvings) and prehistoric ruins.

1. At which site can you see burial mounds shaped like animals?

Effigy Mounds National Monument
_____

2. At which site can you find one of the largest apartment-style houses?

Chaco Canyon Nationai Historical Park
_____

3. At which site can you see petroglyphs? Petrified Forest National Park
_____

4. Which site is not located in the southwestern part of the United States?

Effigy Mounds National Monument
_____

5. Which site is the oldest? Effigy Mounds National Monument
_____

Use after reading Chapter 1, Lesson 3, pages 66–71.

NAME _____ DATE _____

The First AMERICANS

Connect Main Ideas

DIRECTIONS: Use this organizer to show how the environment affected the lives of early people. Write three details to support each main idea.

The First Americans

The Search for Early Peoples

The environment affected the ways early peoples moved from place to place.

1. Student responses may include the formation of the land bridge, the

2. migration of early peoples in search of food, and the effects of physical

3. features on that migration.

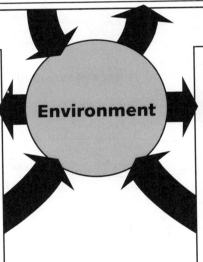

Ancient Indians

The ancient Indians changed their ways of life as the environment changed.

1. Student responses should

show that as the environ-

ment changed and huge

Ice Age animals died out,

2. early peoples began to

fish, to hunt smaller

animals, to gather food,

to farm, and to settle in

3. one place.

Environment

Early Civilizations

Early peoples living in different parts of the Americas had different ways of life.

1. Students should contrast

the lifeways of the Olmecs,

the Mound Builders, and

the Anasazi and relate

2. those lifeways to the

environment in which each

group lived.

3. _____

_____

Use after reading Chapter 1, pages 46–73.

NAME _____ DATE _____

TWO Northwest Coast Indian Canoes

The Northwest Coast Indians used dugout canoes with two different shapes. One type of canoe was built by the Haida. The other was built by the Nootka. Although the canoes were shaped differently, the methods and materials used to make them were the same. Both dugouts were made of cedar. The largest canoes were more than 60 feet (18 m) long and as much as 8 feet (2 m) wide.

Compare Diagrams

DIRECTIONS: Compare the diagrams of the two types of canoes. Then answer the questions that follow.

HAIDA

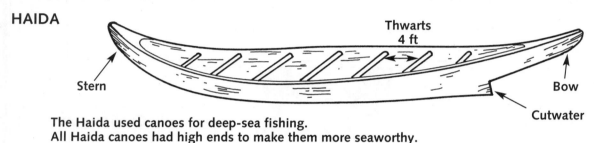

Thwarts
4 ft

Stern

Bow

Cutwater

The Haida used canoes for deep-sea fishing.
All Haida canoes had high ends to make them more seaworthy.

NOOTKA

Thwarts
4 ft

Stern

Bow

Cutwater

The Nootka used canoes for whaling.
All Nootka canoes had a flat strip on the bottom to keep them upright during whale hunts.

1. For what purpose was the Haida canoe used? <u>deep-sea fishing</u>

2. For what purpose was the Nootka canoe used? <u>whaling</u>

3. Look at the bows, or the front ends, of the two canoes. How are they different?
<u>Haida is rounded; Nootka is square.</u>

4. Now compare the sterns, or the back ends, of the two canoes. How are they different?
<u>Haida is curved; Nootka is square and vertical.</u>

5. The thwarts, or braces, that run across the canoes held the canoes' sides in place.
How far apart are the thwarts? <u>4 feet</u>

Use after reading Chapter 2, Lesson 1, pages 75–80.

Harcourt Brace School Publishers

Learning About Kachinas

Compare Visuals

DIRECTIONS: Study the drawings and descriptions of the three kachinas. Then answer the questions that follow.

Sun Kachina

Visits Hopi villages during the bean-planting ceremony. Appeals to the sun for health, happiness, long life, and good crops.

Clown Kachina

Appears during most ceremonies to entertain the crowd. Performs acrobatics, tells jokes, and leads games. Is noisy and silly.

Kachina Mother

Leads the bean-planting ceremony. Is actually a male performer.

1. Which kachina is a spirit of nature? <u>Sun Kachina</u>

2. How can you tell one kind of kachina from another? <u>by the specially painted mask or face</u>

<u>and brightly colored costume</u>

3. Which part of the Sun Kachina's costume represents the sun?

<u>Responses should include reference to the headdress.</u>

4. What makes the Clown Kachina's costume different from the other kachinas' costumes?

<u>Responses may include reference to the Clown Kachina's painted face (instead of a mask),</u>

<u>the boldly striped body, and the horned headdress.</u>

5. Which kachina do you think would play the most important role at the bean-planting

ceremony? Explain. <u>Accept all responses students can reasonably defend.</u>

NAME _____ DATE _____

The Importance of the **BUFFALO**

The buffalo played an important part in the history of our country. As long as the buffalo roamed the Great Plains, the Plains Indians grew in number and strength. The people of the Plains hunted the buffalo for food and used other parts of the animal to make clothing, tools, weapons, and other products.

Interpret Visuals

DIRECTIONS: Study the drawings below, which show the most common buffalo products. Then answer the questions that follow.

BUFFALO PRODUCTS

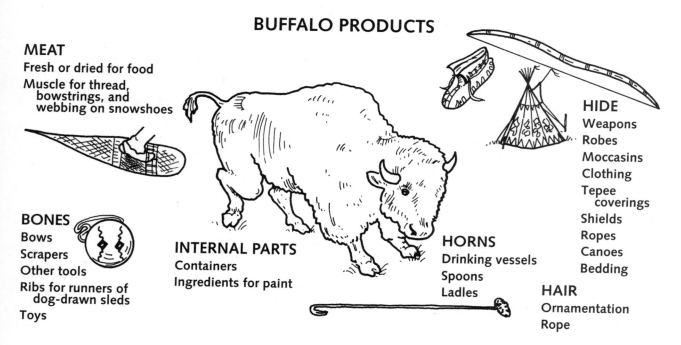

MEAT
Fresh or dried for food
Muscle for thread, bowstrings, and webbing on snowshoes

HIDE
Weapons
Robes
Moccasins
Clothing
Tepee coverings
Shields
Ropes
Canoes
Bedding

BONES
Bows
Scrapers
Other tools
Ribs for runners of dog-drawn sleds
Toys

INTERNAL PARTS
Containers
Ingredients for paint

HORNS
Drinking vessels
Spoons
Ladles

HAIR
Ornamentation
Rope

1. What did the Plains Indians make from the internal parts of the buffalo?
containers and paint

2. Which three parts of the buffalo were used to make different kinds of weapons?
meat, hide, and bones

3. Which part of the buffalo was used to make housing for the Plains Indians?
hides, used to make tepee coverings

4. Which part of the buffalo do you think made the most useful products?
Accept all responses students can reasonably defend.

Use after reading Chapter 2, Lesson 3, pages 86–91.

Harcourt Brace School Publishers

HIAWATHA & Longfellow Make History

Interpret Historical Literature

DIRECTIONS: Study the information about Hiawatha and the lines from Longfellow's poem. Then answer the questions.

Hiawatha, an Onondaga chief, worked hard for peace. In the late 1500s, he persuaded war-weary tribes of the Iroquois nation to stop fighting one another. They united in peace by forming what became known as the Iroquois League.

Hiawatha was believed to have been a shaman, or a religious leader and healer who calls upon the gods to grant the people special favors. He was said to have magical powers. Native American stories describe Hiawatha as a great teacher who taught valuable lessons about farming, hunting, canoeing, medicine, nature, and the arts.

Many years after Hiawatha's death, the stories about Hiawatha inspired Henry Wadsworth Longfellow to write the poem "The Song of Hiawatha." It took Longfellow from June 1854 to March 1855 to write it! You may recognize some verses from this lengthy poem. The lines that follow are from the section about Hiawatha's fasting, a time when he deliberately ate very little or nothing at all.

"You shall hear how Hiawatha
Prayed and fasted in the forest,
Not for greater skill in hunting,
Not for greater craft in fishing,
Not for triumphs in the battle,
And renown [fame] among the warriors,
But for profit of the people,
For advantage of the nations."

1. What was Hiawatha's major accomplishment? He persuaded Iroquois tribes to stop fighting and to unite in peace in the Iroquois League.

2. What is a shaman? a religious leader and healer who calls upon the gods to grant the people special favors

3. Why do you think Longfellow was inspired to write a poem about Hiawatha? Responses may include reference to Hiawatha's magical powers or his accomplishments.

4. According to the poem, what was the purpose of Hiawatha's fasting? He fasted so that good things would come to the people and their nations. Discuss with students Hiawatha's role in forging the Iroquois League.

HOW TO IDENTIFY CAUSES and EFFECTS

Most scientists believe the first Americans crossed over a land bridge from Asia to the Americas. This great migration lasted thousands of years. What was the cause of this great migration? What were the effects?

Apply Critical Thinking Skills

DIRECTIONS: Use the information in Unit 1 about the great migration to complete the following flow chart. Use the flow chart on page 97 of your textbook as a guide.

Accept all reasonable answers. Use the following as a guide.

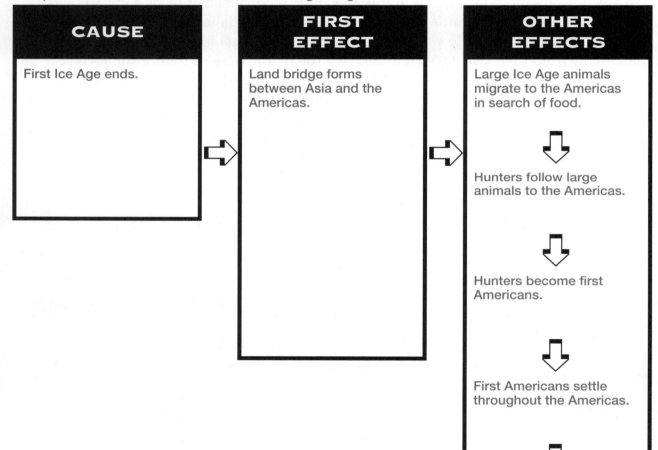

CAUSE	FIRST EFFECT	OTHER EFFECTS
First Ice Age ends.	Land bridge forms between Asia and the Americas.	Large Ice Age animals migrate to the Americas in search of food.
		Hunters follow large animals to the Americas.
		Hunters become first Americans.
		First Americans settle throughout the Americas.
		Early Native American civilizations develop in the Americas.

Harcourt Brace School Publishers

Use after reading Chapter 2, Skill Lesson, page 97.

Unlocking the Mystery of
MAYAN NUMBERS

The Mayas built one of the most well-developed civilizations in the Americas. Their civilization was so highly developed that they had a system for writing and recording time. The Mayas' time system was based on their number system, which used three basic symbols. A shell stood for zero, a dot stood for one, and a bar stood for five.

Recognize Patterns

DIRECTIONS: Study the diagram that shows how the Mayas used three basic symbols in their number system. Then, write the Arabic numerals we would use to write the number that each Mayan symbol or group of symbols represents.

1. __3__ ● ● ●

2. __4__ ● ● ● ●

3. __13__

4. __5__ _____

5. __8__

6. __7__

7. __17__

8. __10__

9. __19__

10. Write your age using the Mayan number system. _____ Answers will vary with students' ages.

Use after reading Chapter 2, Lesson 5, pages 98–103.

NAME _____ DATE _____

Indians OF NORTH AMERICA

Connect Main Ideas

DIRECTIONS: Use this organizer to show the diversity of the ways of life of the American Indians. Write three examples for each cultural region.

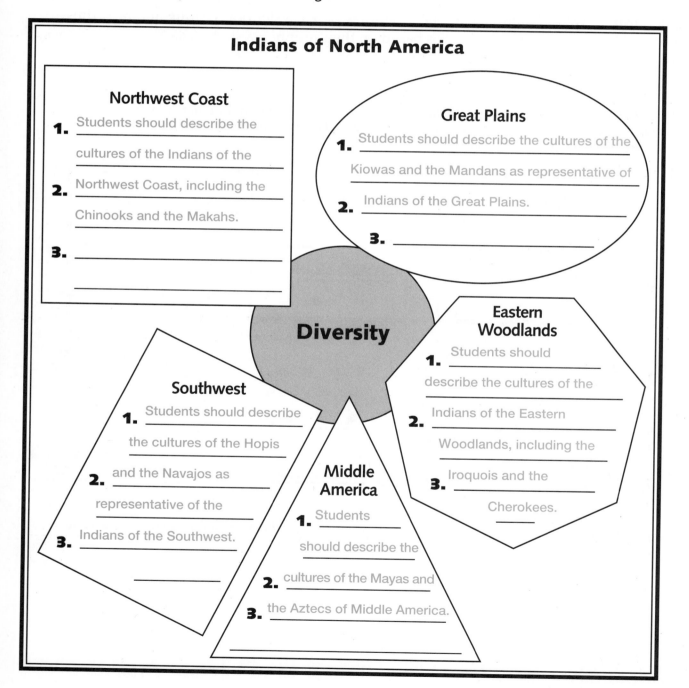

Indians of North America

Northwest Coast

1. Students should describe the _____ cultures of the Indians of the
2. Northwest Coast, including the _____ Chinooks and the Makahs.
3. _____

Great Plains

1. Students should describe the cultures of the _____ Kiowas and the Mandans as representative of
2. Indians of the Great Plains. _____
3. _____

Diversity

Southwest

1. Students should describe _____ the cultures of the Hopis
2. and the Navajos as _____ representative of the
3. Indians of the Southwest. _____

Middle America

1. Students _____ should describe the
2. cultures of the Mayas and _____
3. the Aztecs of Middle America. _____

Eastern Woodlands

1. Students should _____ describe the cultures of the
2. Indians of the Eastern _____ Woodlands, including the
3. Iroquois and the _____ Cherokees.

Use after reading Chapter 2, pages 74–105.

NAME _____ DATE _____

A VIKING SHIP

The Vikings were daring sailors. They set sail without compasses against strong winds and currents. They sailed in open ships such as the one shown below.

Interpret Visuals

DIRECTIONS: Study the diagram below to answer the questions that follow.

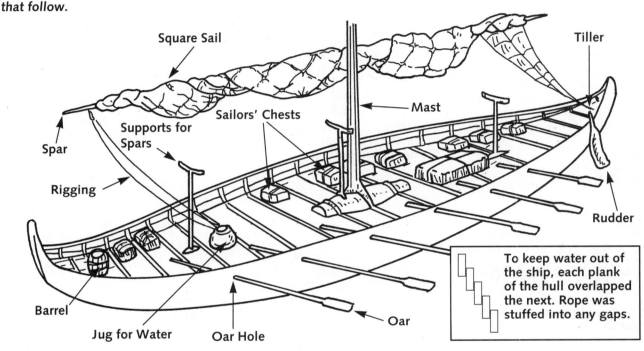

Square Sail

Tiller

Spar

Supports for Spars

Sailors' Chests

Mast

Rigging

Rudder

Barrel

Jug for Water

Oar Hole

Oar

To keep water out of the ship, each plank of the hull overlapped the next. Rope was stuffed into any gaps.

1. How was the Viking ship made watertight? Each plank overlapped the next, and rope was used to plug any gaps.

2. Name two sources of energy that made the ship move. wind for the sails and humans for the oars

3. List three adjectives that describe the Viking ship. Responses may include such adjectives as short, low, dangerous, uncomfortable, unsanitary, open, and small.

4. If you were a Viking, what reasons would you have to set sail in such a ship without a compass or a map to cross the Atlantic Ocean? Accept all reasonable answers, but students should show an appreciation for the Vikings' motivations.

MARCO POLO
and the Riches of Asia

Apply Critical Thinking Skills

**DIRECTIONS: Examine the goods that Marco Polo saw in Asia.
Then complete the following activities.**

Gunpowder

Used in war but
also for fireworks

Number _____

Bookmaking Process

Stamping process used
in China before it was
developed in Europe

Number _____

Saffron

Used for color,
to flavor food,
and as a
natural dye

Number _____

Silk

Silk threads produced by silk-
worms and woven into fabrics

Number _____

"Black Stones"

(believed to be coal)
Used for fuel

Number _____

Jewels

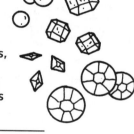

Diamonds,
rubies,
emeralds,
and pearls

Number _____

1. Marco Polo was impressed with things the people in Asia wore. Which of the items above did Asians wear to show their great wealth? silk and jewels

2. In the spaces provided, label the goods from 1 to 6, with 1 being the item you think most encouraged Europeans to find new routes to Asia and 6 being the item you think least encouraged them. Accept all reasonable answers, but students should be able to defend their choices.

3. If you had been a trader in the 1400s, which of the goods would have encouraged you to look for a route to Asia? Explain why you chose this item. Accept all reasonable answers, but students should relate the item to the desire for profit.

Use after reading Chapter 3, Lesson 2, pages 124–129.

Harcourt Brace School Publishers

The Log of
CHRISTOPHER COLUMBUS

Columbus's log shows that he was aware of more than just the sea. His original log, which was given to the king and queen of Spain, was lost. But a copy, passed down from Columbus to his sons and grandson, is our link to Columbus's original log.

Interpret Primary Sources

DIRECTIONS: Read the following accounts from Columbus's log. Then answer the questions that follow.

Thursday, 20 September, 1492. Very early this morning three little birds flew over the ship, singing as they went, and flew away as the sun rose. This was a comforting thought, for unlike the large waterbirds, these little birds could not have come from far off.

Sunday, 23 September, 1492. I saw a dove, a tern, another small river bird and some white birds. . . . The crew is still grumbling about the wind. When I get a wind from the southwest or west it is inconstant, and that, along with a flat sea, has led the men to believe that we will never get home.

Monday, 24 September, 1492. I am having serious trouble with the crew. . . . They have said that it is insanity . . . on their part to risk their lives following the madness of a foreigner. . . . I am told by a few trusted men (and these are few in number!) that if I persist in going onward, the best course of action will be to throw me into the sea some night.

(Reprinted by permission of The McGraw-Hill Companies.)

1. Why was Columbus comforted when he saw the little birds?

because the little birds could not have come far from land

2. Use context clues to find the definition of *inconstant*. In your own words, what does

inconstant mean? Responses will vary, but key words might include changeable, not steady,

unstable, irregular, or not continuous.

3. Why would an inconstant wind make the crew believe that they would not get home?

because a sailing ship is at the mercy of the wind

4. Imagine being on board Columbus's ship. On a separate sheet of paper, rewrite the three entries from Columbus's log as though you were one of the crew.

Responses will vary, but students should describe their feelings as if they were crew members, explain why they feel that way, and write their entries in diary form.

Harcourt Brace School Publishers

HOW TO USE Latitude and Longitude

Columbus was an experienced sailor when he began his search for a new water route to Asia. His first voyage after settling in Portugal appears to have been in early 1477. The map shows some of his other early voyages.

Apply Map and Globe Skills

DIRECTIONS: On the map, study the voyages Columbus made before 1492. Then complete the activities.

1. Columbus set sail from Lisbon on each of his early voyages. Circle this city on the map.

2. What is Lisbon's location? Use longitude and latitude in your answer.
   Accept all answers close to 39°N/9°W.
   _____

3. Put an **X** through Columbus's southernmost landing.

4. Draw a box around the landings that are located between 40°N and 60°N latitude.

5. Historians believe that Columbus landed in Iceland in 1477. At that time most people thought Iceland's northernmost point was at 63°N latitude. Columbus's landing proved otherwise. On the map locate Iceland's northernmost point and write the correct latitude in the space provided.
   66½°N
   _____

6. What name do we give this special parallel? Arctic Circle
   _____

7. Between which two meridians were Columbus's landings? 0° and 30°W
   _____

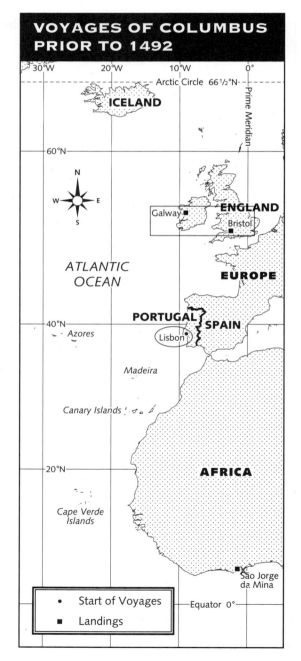

VOYAGES OF COLUMBUS PRIOR TO 1492

Use after reading Chapter 3, Skill Lesson, pages 136–137.

Harcourt Brace School Publishers

The Costs of EXPLORATION

Compare Costs

DIRECTIONS: Read the information below and study the comparison table. Then complete the activities that follow.

How can we understand the costs of Columbus's voyage when prices and values have changed over the centuries? One way is to compare costs by using the value of gold. The maravedi was a copper coin used in Spain in the 1400s. Each maravedi would have about a value of just over 13 cents. The table at the right shows the costs of the first voyage in maravedis and United States dollars.

COSTS OF COLUMBUS'S VOYAGE OF DISCOVERY

	MARAVEDIS	U.S. DOLLARS*
Salaries of all officers	268,000	34,840
Wages of all sailors	252,000	32,760
$ Maintenance	319,680	41,558
Rental cost, *Santa Maria*	172,800	22,464
X Furnishings, arms, trading supplies	155,062	20,158
Total Expenses	**1,167,542**	**151,780**

*maravedis × $0.13 = U.S. dollars

1. Put a dollar sign ($) next to the most expensive part of the voyage. Then put an **X** next to the least expensive part of the voyage.

2. Compare the salaries of the officers and the wages of the sailors. Did it cost more to pay the officers or the sailors? Circle the one that cost more.

3. Columbus offered a reward of 10,000 maravedis to the first person to sight land. What is this amount in U.S. dollars? Students should multiply 10,000 by $0.13, the dollar equivalent, to find the answer: $1,300.

4. The average yearly wage of a sailor on Columbus's voyage was 3,000 maravedis, or $390. Columbus's yearly salary was 50,000 maravedis, or $6,500. If you were a sailor on Columbus's voyage, considering your average yearly wages, would the 10,000 maravedi reward make you want to continue to look for land? (Columbus eventually claimed the reward for himself.) Explain. Responses will vary, but students should compare the $390 yearly wage with the $1,300 reward, which was over three times yearly pay.

Harcourt Brace School Publishers

HOW TO FORM A Logical Conclusion

Columbus died believing that he had reached Asia. Other explorers, however, proved him wrong. Among those explorers were Vespucci, Balboa, and Magellan. These explorers found new facts to prove that Columbus had landed on a different continent.

Apply Critical Thinking Skills

DIRECTIONS: Decide which explorer could have made each statement below. In the space provided, write a V for Vespucci, a B for Balboa, or an M for Magellan. Then draw an X through any statement that does not support the conclusion that these explorers had landed on a different continent.

1. __V__ I found a new way of measuring east and west distances on a map.

2. __M__ I was Portuguese, sailing under the Spanish flag.

3. __M__ I was killed in a fight on the Philippine Islands.

4. __V__ I learned that I had sailed more than three times as far as Columbus thought he had sailed.

5. __M__ Many of my crew died of scurvy and hunger.

6. __B__ I found a huge ocean on the western side of what Columbus had thought was Asia.

7. __B__ I climbed a mountain peak on the Isthmus of Panama.

8. __V__ I studied Ptolemy's work and found that if Asia were as far east as Columbus had thought, it would cover half the Earth.

9. __V__ In the areas I explored, I saw no evidence of what Marco Polo had seen in Asia.

10. __M__ I found that you could reach Asia by sailing west around the world.

11. __B__ I supported Vespucci's findings by crossing the Isthmus of Panama.

12. __M__ My ships sailed for more than three months across the Pacific.

13. __B__ My exploring party included Spanish and African soldiers.

14. __M__ I set sail in September 1519.

Use after reading Chapter 3, Skill Lesson, page 145.

The Age of
Exploration

Connect Main Ideas

DIRECTIONS: Use this organizer to show how new information helped Europeans gain knowledge and explore the unknown. Write three details for each lesson.

The Age of Exploration

A Legendary Land

1. People told stories about unknown lands. They thought the world outside the
2. place they lived was dangerous. Square-sailed ships made ocean travel very
hard, and there were not many maps. European rulers did not want to spend their
3. time or money sending ships beyond Europe's borders.

New Information

Background to European Exploration

1. Marco Polo returned to Europe with pockets full of jewels and with stories about
2. the wealth of Asia. Advances in technology led to faster sailing ships and better
3. navigation instruments, such as the compass. Constantinople was closed to
traders, so Europeans had good reason to find a new route to Asia.

New Information

I, Columbus: My Journal 1492–1493

1. Spain's monarchs agreed to pay for Columbus's journey to Asia so they could spread
2. Christianity. In return, Columbus promised them great wealth and that Christianity
3. would be spread to the people of Asia.

New Information

Early Voyages of Exploration

1. Vespucci did not believe Columbus had reached Asia because Columbus had found neither
2. cities of gold and marble nor people wearing cloth of gold. Vespucci studied the writings of
3. Marco Polo and Ptolemy. He learned that the Earth was larger and Asia was smaller than previously thought. Eventually, other explorers traveled even farther than Columbus. Balboa reached the Pacific Ocean. Magellan was the first to sail around the world.

Harcourt Brace School Publishers

A Day in TENOCHTITLÁN

What was it like to live in the Aztec capital of Tenochtitlán before it was conquered by Cortés? Here is an account of what a typical day for a male citizen in that city might have been like.

Compare Cultures

DIRECTIONS: Read the story about daily life in Tenochtitlán. Complete the table that follows to compare your daily life with that of an Aztec living in Tenochtitlán.

The merchant's guild has accepted me as a member. I am now ready to travel with a caravan of my own. How my life will change!

The temple trumpets guide the daily routine in Tenochtitlán. My stucco house has one bedroom for the whole family, one other small room, a bathroom, and no furniture except mats. At sunrise the sound of the temple trumpets wakes me and I bathe, put on my loin cloth, pick up food to eat later, and go to work. Before long I hear the trumpets again. Then I take the day's first meal and return to work. At about the time the sun is directly overhead, the trumpets signal me to return home to eat and to take a brief nap. After my nap, I go back to work until nightfall, when the trumpets sound the end of the workday.

At the end of the workday, I go home and spend time with my family until the trumpets blow again. Then I know it is time to go to sleep.

	YOU	AZTEC
Wake-Up Time	Responses will vary but should reflect students' lives.	sunrise
Housing		stucco house, one bedroom, one other small room, bathroom; no furniture except for mats
Meals		midmorning break for first meal; midday lunch
Work		work from early morning to midmorning and after a break, work until midday; return to work after lunch and nap; work until nightfall

Harcourt Brace School Publishers

Use after reading Chapter 4, Lesson 1, pages 149–153.

Estéban in Time and Place

Sequence Events

DIRECTIONS: Read the following quotations about Estéban, also known as Estevanico. Place the events discussed in the proper sequence by numbering the passages from 1 to 5, with 1 being the first event and 5 the last. Then use the information to answer the questions that follow.

___2___ "In 1538 Governor Mendoza organized an expedition to discover this land of great wealth and picked Father Marcos de Niza, a Franciscan friar, to lead it. Estevanico was his advance scout and advisor." *William Loren Katz*

___3___ "Estevanico traveled ahead of the main group, taking only a few Indians with him. The Indians could not speak Spanish, so Estevanico agreed to send Friar Marcos a cross made of twigs or tree branches to report his findings. A small cross would mean he had found nothing out of the ordinary. But if he found great cities he would send back a large cross." *Sibyl Hancock*

___5___ "Some historians, unfriendly toward the African, . . . [believe] he was murdered. One scholar believes Estevanico died for claiming to represent a powerful white country to Indians. Some historians have wondered if the young slave saw an opportunity for freedom and took it." *William Loren Katz*

___1___ "Not too much is known of his [Estéban's] early life. Born in Azamore, Morocco, around 1500, he was probably made captive as a teenager when Portugal's King Manoel seized the city in 1513." *William Loren Katz*

___4___ "[Estéban] . . . proceeded into the interior and sent back wooden crosses to indicate his progress. When his crosses increased in size until they were as tall as a man, the Spaniards realized that the [African] explorer had experienced great success. Indians brought news of Little Stephen's [Estéban's] approach to the fabulous seven cities about which so much had been heard." *John Hope Franklin*

1. In what country was Estéban born? _Morocco_____

2. Who was chosen to lead the expedition? _Father Marcos de Niza_____

3. List all of Estéban's jobs. _advance scout, advisor, explorer_____

4. Reread Katz's different descriptions of Estéban's death. On a separate sheet of paper, write your own ending to the story of Estéban's search for the Seven Cities of Gold.
Answers should be supported by facts presented here and in the textbook.

Do You Speak *Spanish?*

Understand Word Origins

DIRECTIONS: Study the information in the dictionary box below. Use your textbook to help you fill in the blanks in the box. Then answer the questions that follow.

---

alligator came to English through Spanish. The Spanish word for "alligator" is *lagarto*. The Spanish word for "the" is *el*. When English speakers heard *el lagarto,* it sounded to them like "alligator."

armadillo a Spanish word meaning "armed man," or "little armored one." This word describes an animal whose body is almost entirely protected by an armorlike covering.

conquistador
_____ comes from the Spanish word meaning "one who conquers by physical, mental, or moral force."

Florida
_____ a state name that comes from the Spanish word meaning "filled with flowers."

mosquito a Spanish and Portuguese word that means "little fly."

parakeet comes from the Spanish *periquito* and the Old French *paroquet,* both meaning "parrot."

---

1. What part of speech are all of these words? _____ nouns _____

2. Which word came to English through a misunderstanding? _alligator_____

3. Which words came to English from two different languages? _mosquito, parakeet_____

4. Which Spanish word is the name of a state? _Florida_____

5. On a separate sheet of paper, make a list of all the words you know that come from Spanish. Possible answers include rodeo, ranch, lariat, and bananas.

6. On the same sheet of paper, make a table with the following headings: ANIMALS, PEOPLE, PLACES. Write the words from the dictionary box and the words from the list you made for question 5 under the proper headings. Circle the category heading under which you have the most words. Students should make a table and classify the words above under three headings—ANIMALS: alligator, armadillo, mosquito, parakeet; PEOPLE: conquistador; PLACES: Florida—as well as the words on their own lists. Students should circle the category heading under which they have the most words.

Use after reading Chapter 4, Lesson 3, pages 159–163.

Harcourt Brace School Publishers

NAME _____ DATE _____

HOW TO USE A MAP to Show Movement

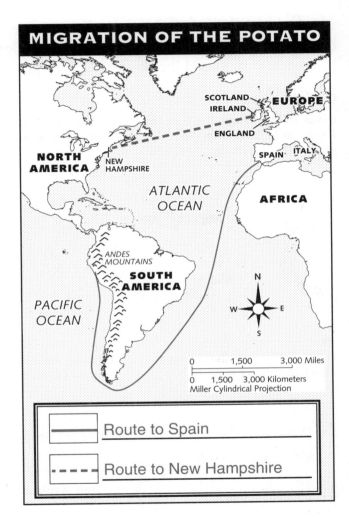

MIGRATION OF THE POTATO

Apply Map and Globe Skills

DIRECTIONS: Read the following paragraph and study the map. Then complete the activities below.

Potatoes were first grown by Inca Indians living in the Andes Mountains in northwestern South America. Spanish explorers in South America brought potatoes back to Spain. From Spain, potatoes were taken to Italy and England.

The English introduced the potato to Ireland and Scotland. Although English colonists brought potatoes to the colonies as early as 1621, potatoes did not become an important crop until the Irish immigrants brought them to New Hampshire in 1719.

1. Imagine that you are a Spanish explorer. You have just set sail from an area near the Andes Mountains of South America. You are sailing south on the Pacific Ocean. Draw in red the route that you will follow to sail back to Spain.

2. Imagine that you are an Irish immigrant. You have just arrived in New Hampshire. Draw in blue the route that you followed as you sailed from Ireland to New Hampshire.

3. In the spaces provided, use the same two colors to make a map key to explain the information shown on your map.

Harcourt Brace School Publishers

Preparing
Furs for Trade

The French bartered with the American Indians, exchanging European goods for beaver furs. At first the French did not hunt the beavers. American Indians trapped the beavers and prepared the beaver skins, or pelts, for trade.

Read a Flow Chart

DIRECTIONS: Study the flow chart that shows the steps American Indians followed to tan and cure beaver skins. Then answer the questions that follow.

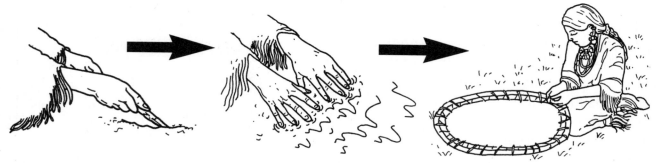

Step 1
Scraping: Scraping the pelt with a stick to clean it

Step 2
Tanning: Rubbing the pelt with marrow (sticky center of bone)

Step 3
Curing: Drying the scraped and tanned pelt on a stretching frame

1. What was the first step in preparing the beaver skins for trade?
scraping the pelt clean

2. Describe the tanning process. Pelt is rubbed with marrow.

3. What was the final step in preparing the hide for trade? curing, or drying tanned pelt on
stretching frame

4. Rewrite these steps in the correct order: tanning, scraping, curing.
scraping, tanning, curing

Harcourt Brace School Publishers

HARVEST FESTIVALS

Was the Pilgrims' Thanksgiving the first Thanksgiving? You already know that there are many ideas about the first Thanksgiving in the Americas. What about the rest of the world? People around the world have held harvest festivals since they first harvested crops.

Compare Holiday Celebrations

DIRECTIONS: Study the chart below to learn about harvest festivals around the world. Next, complete the chart by filling in the information for the United States. Then use the chart to complete the activities that follow.

HARVEST FESTIVALS

PLACE	NAME OF FESTIVAL	WHEN HELD	FESTIVITIES
India	In honor of Gauri, goddess of the harvest and women	September	Offerings of milk and sweets to Gauri; feasting
Israel	Sukkot (also called the Feast of Tabernacles)	Autumn	Special shelters called succahs or tabernacles are built
Ancient China	Hhung-Ch'iu (the birthday of the moon)	Fifteenth day of the eighth month	Round moon cakes and round fruits on altars
England	Harvest Home	Harvest time; autumn	Feasting on roast beef, pudding; songs
Inca Empire	The Song of the Harvest	May (autumn in Southern Hemisphere)	Offering of first corn to their gods
United States	Thanksgiving	Accept autumn, fall, November, fourth Thursday in November.	Answers should describe what students know of U.S. holiday.

1. During which season of the year are most harvest festivals held?

Accept autumn or fall.

2. Why do you think the Incas celebrated their harvest festival in May?

They lived in the Southern Hemisphere, which has seasons opposite to ours; May was their harvest

time, during their autumn.

3. On a separate sheet of paper, describe what you think would be the perfect Thanksgiving Day celebration, from the beginning of the day to the end.

Accept all reasonable descriptions.

Use after reading Chapter 4, Lesson 5, pages 171–177.

HOW TO READ Parallel Time Lines

Apply Chart and Graph Skills

DIRECTIONS: The parallel time lines below list events that happened in many different places. Study the time lines and then answer the questions that follow.

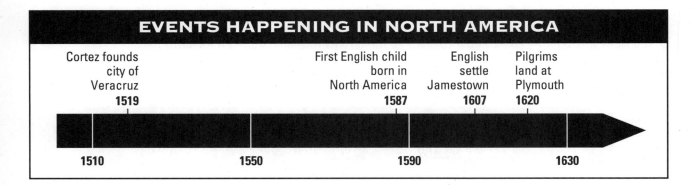

EVENTS HAPPENING IN NORTH AMERICA

Cortez founds city of Veracruz **1519**

First English child born in North America **1587**

English settle Jamestown **1607**

Pilgrims land at Plymouth **1620**

1510   **1550**   **1590**   **1630**

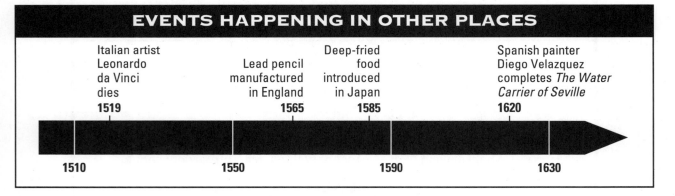

EVENTS HAPPENING IN OTHER PLACES

Italian artist Leonardo da Vinci dies **1519**

Lead pencil manufactured in England **1565**

Deep-fried food introduced in Japan **1585**

Spanish painter Diego Velazquez completes *The Water Carrier of Seville* **1620**

1510   **1550**   **1590**   **1630**

1. In which year did the English settle Jamestown? <u>1607</u>

2. Which event occurred first—Diego Velazquez's completion of *The Water Carrier of Seville* or Leonardo da Vinci's death? <u>**Leonardo da Vinci's death**</u>

3. Was the first lead pencil manufactured in England before or after the first English child was born in North America? <u>**before**</u>

4. What was happening in North America in the same year that Diego Velazquez completed *The Water Carrier of Seville*? <u>**Pilgrims landed at Plymouth.**</u>

Use after reading Chapter 4, Skill Lesson, pages 178–179.

NAME _____ DATE _____

Encounters in the Americas

Connect Main Ideas

DIRECTIONS: Use this organizer to show how the chapter's main
ideas are connected. Write the main idea of each lesson.

Conquest of the Aztecs and Incas

The Spaniards' desire for

gold and other riches led

to fighting between the

Spanish and the Aztecs

and the Spanish and the

Incas during the 1500s.

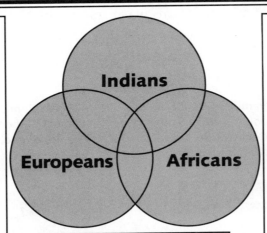

Indians

Europeans   Africans

Encounters in the Americas

The English in the Americas

Cooperation with the

Indians and with one

another helped the

English colonists survive

at Jamestown and

Plymouth.

The Search for Gold and Riches

The Spanish explored North

America in the 1500s

because they wanted to add

to their empire and were

eager for gold and other

riches.

New People in America

The Spanish came to the

Americas to make native

peoples Christians, to find

the wealth they had heard

about, and to settle the land.

Africans were brought to the

Americas as slaves to do

work.

Encounters with the French and Dutch

The fur trade brought wealth

to the French and the Dutch

and enabled the Indians to

trade furs for useful goods.

The fur trade made the

French less interested in

establishing colonies and

caused the Indians to lose

land and fight intertribal wars.

Use after reading Chapter 4, pages 148–181.

Comparing Spanish Missions

The mission of San Antonio de Valero was built by the Catholic Church in what is now Texas. This mission was later given a new name—Pueblo del Alamo, later known as the Alamo.

Understand Diagrams

DIRECTIONS: Compare the diagram below with the diagram of a Spanish mission shown on pages 198–199 in your textbook. Write an **S** next to each statement that describes a Spanish mission. Write an **A** next to each statement that describes the Alamo. Write **SA** next to each statement that describes both missions.

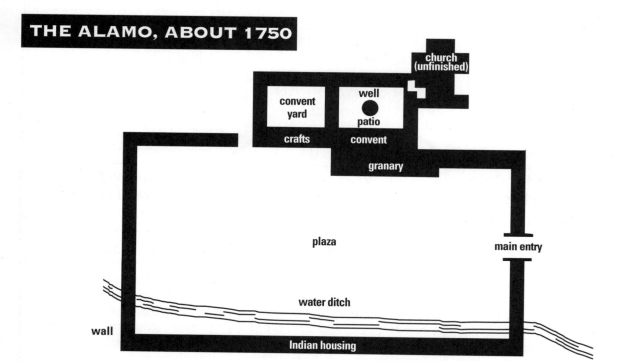

THE ALAMO, ABOUT 1750

SA water source outside mission

A all crafts contained within mission walls

SA large, open area in center of mission

SA mission includes a church

SA missionaries housed inside mission

S ranch workers housed outside mission

SA walls surround entire mission

SA patio within mission walls

a taste of
LOUISIANA

Apply Reading and Research Skills

DIRECTIONS: Study the list of words in the box and read the passage about Louisiana below. Then write the correct word for each numbered blank on the lines following the passage.

Welcome to Louisiana, a spicy, southern state splashed by the waters of the Gulf of Mexico. Water dominates Louisiana. Slow-moving streams known as **1** are common sights. The Mississippi River carries millions of tons of sediment, or sand and soil, into the Gulf of Mexico and deposits it at the mouth of the river, forming a delta. The Mississippi Delta covers about one-fourth of the state. The average Louisiana resident lives on land that is five feet below sea level. Wetlands throughout Louisiana are home to many kinds of wildlife. Herons, bald eagles, and brown pelicans thrive there. Millions of ducks, geese, and other birds winter in Louisiana. But the state is more than colorful geographic features and birds. A multicultural spirit flavors Louisiana! Treat yourself to the flavorful local foods by eating a hot bowl of **2** or a spicy rice dish of **3**. As you eat, listen for the street-side musicians playing toe-tapping **4**. Visit New Orleans, where jazz was born, and join in one of the many music festivals.

In New Orleans, excitement is in the air. People in the street chat about the upcoming **5**, a fun-filled celebration of music, costumes, and parades. Louisiana natives come from all over the state to join in this celebration.

A DICTIONARY OF LOUISIANA

bayous   slow-moving streams

gumbo   a spicy soup made with a mixture of vegetables, meat, seafood, and sassafras leaves

jambalaya   spicy rice cooked with seafood or meat

Mardi Gras   a day of merrymaking and carnival

zydeco   a type of music that combines rock and roll with Cajun and African American sounds

1. bayous _____

2. gumbo _____

3. jambalaya _____

4. zydeco _____

5. Mardi Gras _____

Use after reading Chapter 5, Lesson 2, pages 201–205.

THE ROUTES OF
THREE COLONISTS

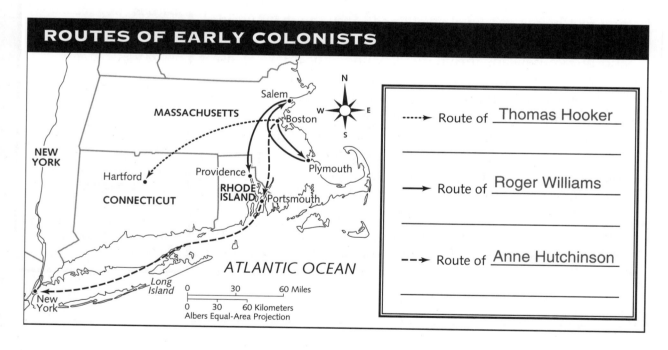

Apply Map and Globe Skills

DIRECTIONS: Read the following descriptions of three early colonists and study the map. Complete the map key by writing the names of the colonists in the blanks next to their route lines. Then use the map scale to complete the statements below the map.

Roger Williams arrived in Boston from England in 1631. The following year he moved to Plymouth. In 1633 he moved to Salem. In 1636 Williams traveled to Rhode Island, where he founded the town of Providence.

Thomas Hooker sailed to New England in 1633 and settled near Boston. In 1636 Hooker and a group of followers moved to Connecticut, where they founded Hartford.

Anne Hutchinson came to Boston in 1634. She was sent away from Massachusetts for criticizing the beliefs of the Puritans who lived there. In 1638 she founded Portsmouth, a new settlement in Rhode Island. The Hutchinson family later moved to Long Island and finally settled in New York.

ROUTES OF EARLY COLONISTS

Salem
MASSACHUSETTS
Boston
NEW YORK
Hartford
Providence
CONNECTICUT
RHODE ISLAND
Portsmouth
Plymouth
Long Island
New York
ATLANTIC OCEAN

0   30   60 Miles
0   30   60 Kilometers
Albers Equal-Area Projection

- - - - → Route of __Thomas Hooker__

————→ Route of __Roger Williams__

– – → Route of __Anne Hutchinson__

1. The distance between Boston and Plymouth is about __30__ miles.

2. When Hooker and his followers left Boston for Hartford, they traveled about __90__ miles.

Use after reading Chapter 5, Lesson 3, pages 206–210.

NAME _____ DATE _____

The MIDDLE COLONIES

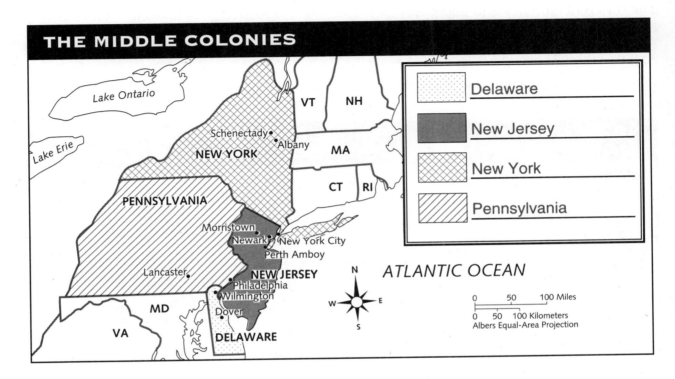

Apply Map and Globe Skills

DIRECTIONS: Lightly color each of the middle colonies shown on the map, using a different color for each colony. Then use the same colors to make a key for the map.

DIRECTIONS: Match each colony to its major cities by writing the name of the colony in the blank beside each city name.

1. Dover, _Delaware_

2. Schenectady, _New York_

3. Morristown, _New Jersey_

4. Lancaster, _Pennsylvania_

5. Wilmington, _Delaware_

6. Perth Amboy, _New Jersey_

7. New York City, _New York_

8. Albany, _New York_

9. Philadelphia, _Pennsylvania_

10. Newark, _New Jersey_

Harcourt Brace School Publishers

Comparing *the Colonies*

The English colonies in America were generally founded by settlers from Europe. These European settlers established colonies in three regions, each of which developed its own way of life. Each group that came to the colonies contributed its own specific skills. The different climates and geographical resources also helped people decide which industries to build and which crops to raise.

Apply Critical Thinking Skills

DIRECTIONS: Study the maps and the table below. Then answer the questions on page 35.

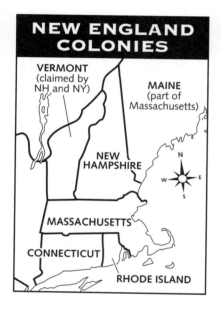
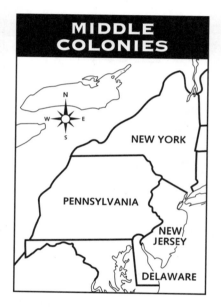
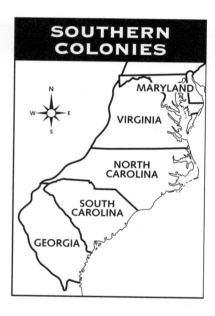

	NEW ENGLAND COLONIES	MIDDLE COLONIES	SOUTHERN COLONIES
Settlers	English	Dutch, English, French, German, Scotch-Irish, free Africans	English, Scots, French, African slaves
Geography	pine and hardwood forests, poor rocky soil, good coastal harbors, swift unnavigable rivers	hardwood forests, good coastal harbors, fertile soil, large navigable rivers	pine and hardwood forests, good coastal harbors, fertile soil, wetlands, navigable rivers
Major Industries	shipbuilding, whaling, trading, fishing	flour milling, farming, shipping, trading, rifle making	trading, farming
Major Crops	corn, barley, wheat, rye, flax	wheat	tobacco, rice, indigo, cotton, corn, wheat

(continued)

Use after reading Chapter 5, Lesson 5, pages 218–224.

Harcourt Brace School Publishers

1. Which farm crops raised in the southern colonies were not raised in the other colonies?

   tobacco, rice, indigo, and cotton

2. What made it possible for trade with Europe to be an important industry in all three groups of colonies?

   good coastal harbors

3. Which group of colonies probably had the poorest system of river transportation?

   New England colonies

4. Which colonies attracted settlers from the largest number of countries?

   middle colonies

5. Whale oil was very popular because it burned cleaner and brighter than candles. To which group of colonies would you have gone to find whale oil?

   New England colonies

6. Only the southern colonies could grow rice. What geographical feature of the southern colonies was good for growing rice?

   wetlands

7. The middle colonies were called the "breadbasket colonies" because they grew mostly wheat. What industry in the middle colonies was directly related to wheat farming?

   flour milling

8. What did the major industries in the New England colonies seem to have in common?

   They all relied upon the good coastal harbors.

9. How were the geographical features of the New England colonies related to these industries?

   The pine and hardwood forests would be used in shipbuilding. Access to a coastal harbor would be needed for whaling and trading and fishing.

HOW TO Classify INFORMATION

Although the colonists lived in the Americas, they still thought of themselves as Spanish, Dutch, French, English, or African, depending on where they came from. These colonists brought with them the languages and customs of their homelands, and these languages and customs became part of our history. Their influences can still be seen throughout the United States today.

Apply Critical Thinking Skills

DIRECTIONS: Examine the terms shown below. Then decide whether each term is most closely related to the Spanish, French, or English colonists. Write the term under the name of the appropriate category.

Juan Ponce de León	Des Moines	San Antonio	Puritans
Sir Francis Drake	El Camino Real	Code Noir	Quakers
King George II	Florida	hacienda	mission
La Salle	Jamestown	Huguenots	The Virginia
King Louis XIV	Louisiana	indigo	Company
St. Augustine	New Orleans	portage	Fundamental
Pedro Menéndez de Avilés	Quebec	presidio	Orders

SPANISH	FRENCH	ENGLISH
Juan Ponce de León	La Salle	Sir Francis Drake
Pedro Menéndez de Avilés	King Louis XIV	King George II
El Camino Real	Des Moines	Jamestown
Florida	Louisiana	Puritans
San Antonio	New Orleans	Quakers
hacienda	Quebec	The Virginia Company
presidio	Code Noir	indigo
mission	Huguenots	Fundamental Orders
St. Augustine	portage	

Harcourt Brace School Publishers

NAME _____ DATE _____

Europeans Settle Throughout
NORTH AMERICA

Connect Main Ideas

**DIRECTIONS: Use this organizer to show how the chapter's
main ideas are connected. Write three examples to support
each main idea.**

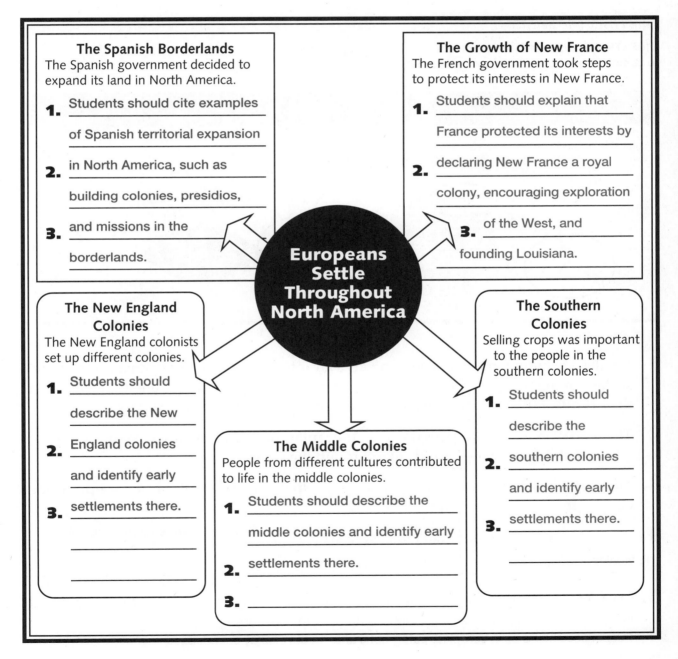

The Spanish Borderlands
The Spanish government decided to
expand its land in North America.

1. Students should cite examples

   of Spanish territorial expansion

2. in North America, such as

   building colonies, presidios,

3. and missions in the

   borderlands.

The Growth of New France
The French government took steps
to protect its interests in New France.

1. Students should explain that

   France protected its interests by

2. declaring New France a royal

   colony, encouraging exploration

3. of the West, and

   founding Louisiana.

**The New England
Colonies**
The New England colonists
set up different colonies.

1. Students should

   describe the New

2. England colonies

   and identify early

3. settlements there.

**Europeans
Settle
Throughout
North America**

**The Southern
Colonies**
Selling crops was important
to the people in the
southern colonies.

1. Students should

   describe the

2. southern colonies

   and identify early

3. settlements there.

The Middle Colonies
People from different cultures contributed
to life in the middle colonies.

1. Students should describe the

   middle colonies and identify early

2. settlements there.

3. _____

Having a WHALE of a Time

New London, Connecticut; New Bedford, Massachusetts; and Sag Harbor, New York, were once important whaling centers. By the 1970s whalers had killed so many whales that many species were near extinction. In 1972 the United States Marine Mammal Protection Act stopped the widespread slaughter of whales by United States citizens. Many other countries have passed similar laws.

Link History to Science

DIRECTIONS: Use the information above and the diagram below to complete the activities following the diagram.

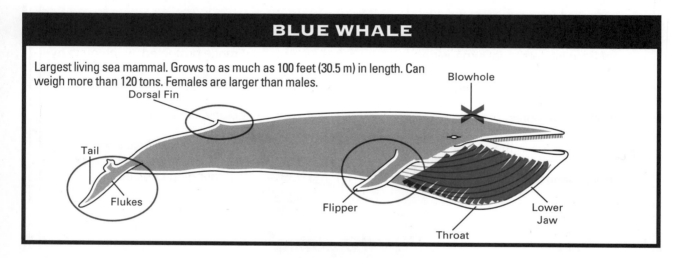

BLUE WHALE

Largest living sea mammal. Grows to as much as 100 feet (30.5 m) in length. Can weigh more than 120 tons. Females are larger than males.

Dorsal Fin

Blowhole

Tail

Flukes

Flipper

Throat

Lower Jaw

1. Whales are mammals that need to breathe air into their lungs. They must come to the surface of the water every few minutes to breathe. Whales' nostrils are in the top of their heads. Put an **X** over the part of the whale where you would find its nostrils.

2. The blue whale travels at speeds up to 15$\frac{1}{2}$ miles per hour. Circle each part of the whale that helps it balance and steer through the water.

3. The blue whale has grooves on its throat that help it trap mouthfuls of "sea soup." Shade or color this part of the whale.

4. Why was the Marine Mammal Protection Act passed? **to stop the widespread slaughter of whales**

5. On a separate sheet of paper, write a paragraph explaining why you do or do not think it is important to pass laws that protect whales from hunters.
Responses should be in complete paragraphs and should display sound reasoning.

Use after reading Chapter 6, Lesson 1, pages 229–233.

HOW TO READ a Circle Graph

Apply Chart and Graph Skills

DIRECTIONS: *The circle graph below shows how the population of New York State was divided in 1800. Study the graph and then answer the questions that follow.*

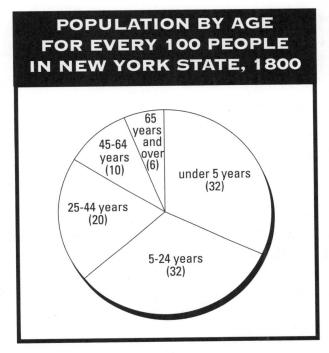

**POPULATION BY AGE
FOR EVERY 100 PEOPLE
IN NEW YORK STATE, 1800**

65 years and over (6)
45-64 years (10)
under 5 years (32)
25-44 years (20)
5-24 years (32)

1. In 1800, for every 100 people in New York State, how many were between the ages of 25 and 44? 20 _____

2. What was the smallest age group in New York State? 65 years and over (6) _____

3. Which were the largest age groups in New York State in 1800? under 5 years (32) and 5–24 years (32) _____

4. For every 100 people, which was larger: the age group 25–44 years or the combined age groups of 45–64 years and 65 years and over? the age group 25–44 years _____

5. For every 100 people, was the population of those aged 24 years and younger more than or less than half of the overall population of New York State in 1800? more than half of the population _____

Use after reading Chapter 6, Skill Lesson, page 234.

Looking at Life in the Southern Colonies

Do you think you would be ready at age 17 to take over the business of three plantations? Eliza Lucas did just that. She did not have a choice. The Lucas family moved from the West Indies to South Carolina when Eliza was 16 years old. Soon after her father went off to fight a war, her mother fell seriously ill and Eliza was left in charge.

Describe Life on a Plantation

DIRECTIONS: Study Eliza Lucas's own words. Try to understand her daily life. Then write E next to each statement that describes Eliza's life.

After being left in charge of the plantations, Eliza wrote the following to a friend in England:

"I have the business of three plantations to transact . . . [which] requires much writing and more business and fatigue of other sorts than you can imagine. "

After experiencing what it was like to run the three plantations, Eliza wrote of her daily routine:

"I rise at five o'clock in the morning, read till seven, then take a walk in the garden or fields, see that the servants are at their respective business. . . . The first hour after breakfast is spent at music, the next is constantly employed in recollecting something I have learned, such as French or shorthand."

__E__ **1.** I am tired from all the writing and business that is part of managing three plantations.

_____ **2.** I have basically the same daily routine as other teenagers.

__E__ **3.** I spend much of the early morning reading.

__E__ **4.** It is important to remember what you read and learn.

_____ **5.** No teenager is able to take charge of a business.

_____ **6.** I spend my whole day working and have no time for fun.

__E__ **7.** It is important to be up before sunrise.

_____ **8.** Taking a walk in the garden or fields is a waste of time.

DIRECTIONS: On a separate sheet of paper, write a brief description of your daily routine. How does your daily routine compare to Eliza Lucas's? Do you see life the same way?

Accept all reasonable answers, but be sure students compare their daily routines to that of Eliza Lucas.

Use after reading Chapter 6, Lesson 2, pages 235–240.

TOOLING Around the Frontier

Sequence with Visuals

DIRECTIONS: *The diagram below shows how the broadax was used to make lumber to build cabins. Study the diagram. Then place the steps on the right in the proper sequence by numbering them from 1 through 10.*

USING THE BROADAX TO MAKE LUMBER

Step 1 Making chalk line on bark-stripped log. Four chalk lines are made by "twanging" a chalked cord onto log to square off log.

Chalk Line

Step 2 Scoring to chalk line. Stand on log and hold long-handled felling ax. Use felling ax to make deep vertical cuts up to chalk line. This is known as "scoring."

Dog
Felling Ax

Step 3 Hewing to chalk line. Stand alongside log. Hold broadax with two hands. Place one knee next to log. Use broadax to hew, or split off, the vertical cuts made in Step 2.

Broadax

___2___ Strip bark.

___4___ Snap chalk lines.

___9___ Hew log to chalk lines.

___6___ Stand on log and hold felling ax.

___1___ Fell, or cut down, tree.

___8___ Stand next to log and hold broadax.

___5___ Place "dog" to hold log.

___7___ Make vertical cuts in log.

___3___ Place chalk lines on log.

___10___ Notch ends of log to use to build cabin.

Harcourt Brace School Publishers

Use after reading Chapter 6, Lesson 3, pages 241–245.

NAME _____ DATE _____

HOW TO USE a Product Map
to Make Generalizations

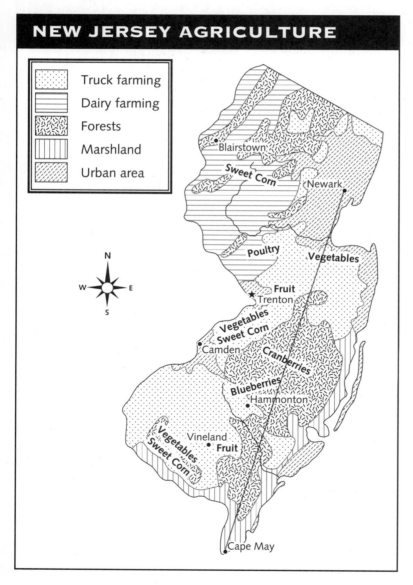

Apply Map and Globe Skills

DIRECTIONS: Use the map below to complete the following activities.

NEW JERSEY AGRICULTURE

Legend:
- Truck farming
- Dairy farming
- Forests
- Marshland
- Urban area

(Map labels: Blairstown, Sweet Corn, Newark, Poultry, Vegetables, Fruit, Trenton, Vegetables, Sweet Corn, Camden, Cranberries, Blueberries, Hammonton, Vegetables, Sweet Corn, Vineland, Fruit, Cape May)

1. Draw a line from Newark to Cape May. Identify the different areas you would pass through if you traveled from north to south along this line.

urban areas, truck farming,

forests, and marshland

2. What city in New Jersey is located in the area where cranberries and blueberries are grown?

Hammonton

3. What is the main use of land around Vineland?

truck farming

4. What crop grows in most parts of New Jersey?

sweet corn

5. Would you be more likely to be a farmer if you lived in Vineland, Cape May, or Newark?

Vineland

Use after reading Chapter 6, Skill Lesson, pages 246–247.

LIFE IN THE
BRITISH COLONIES

Connect Main Ideas

DIRECTIONS: Use this organizer to compare the ways of life of early colonists. Write three examples for each place.

**Life in
Towns
and
Cities**

1. New England towns had meetinghouses and commons; governed by town meetings
2. in market towns farmers could trade their produce for goods and services
3. county seats were the main towns of many counties and the centers of county governments

most coastal cities had good harbors and grew because of trade; centers for businesses

**Life
in the
British Colonies**

**Life on
Plantations**

1. plantation owners

2. people who worked on plantations without pay for a certain length of time to pay back the planters

3. plantation workers who were enslaved for life with no hope of gaining freedom

**Life
on
the
Frontier**

1. attacks by wild animals as well as human enemies, including the Indians, the French, and the Spanish

2. clearing the land; planting crops; cutting timber for homes; gathering and cooking food

3. _____

HISTORICAL EVENTS
OF THE 1700s

Apply Chart and Graph Skills

DIRECTIONS: Write the number of each event at the correct place on the time line. Be sure to place the number of the event at the correct date and on the correct side of the time line.

1. **1755** Earthquake shocks Lisbon, Portugal, killing at least 10,000 people
2. **1747** Virginia settlers and Pennsylvania traders move into Ohio Territory
3. **1760** Daniel Boone hired to scout the frontier in present-day eastern Tennessee
4. **1755** British drive French settlers out of Acadia
5. **1749** Philadelphia founds what becomes the University of Pennsylvania
6. **1726** Jonathan Swift's novel, *Gulliver's Travels*, is an instant success in Europe
7. **1750** Johann Sebastian Bach, the great composer, dies in Germany
8. **1763** Proclamation of 1763 bans settlement west of the Appalachian Mountains
9. **1753** French in Canada move into British lands in Ohio River valley
10. **1718** Pirate known as Blackbeard killed in sea battle off North Carolina coast
11. **1759** British win Battle of Quebec, capturing city
12. **1754** Opening battle of French and Indian War
13. **1763** The French and Indian War ends
14. **1756** British declare war on French in Europe, starting the Seven Years' War

Use after reading Chapter 7, Lesson 1, pages 263–267.

HOW TO USE A Historical Map

Apply Map and Globe Skills

DIRECTIONS:
The map on this page shows where some large immigrant groups were concentrated during the colonial period. Study the map. Then answer the questions that follow.

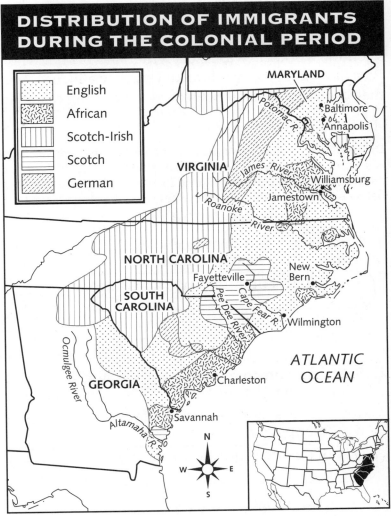

DISTRIBUTION OF IMMIGRANTS DURING THE COLONIAL PERIOD

English
African
Scotch-Irish
Scotch
German

MARYLAND
Baltimore
Annapolis
VIRGINIA
Potomac R.
James River
Williamsburg
Jamestown
Roanoke River
NORTH CAROLINA
Fayetteville
New Bern
SOUTH CAROLINA
Cape Fear R.
Pee Dee River
Wilmington
Ocmulgee River
GEORGIA
Charleston
ATLANTIC OCEAN
Savannah
Altamaha R.

1. Which immigrant group settled farthest west? ___Scotch-Irish___

2. Which immigrant group settled farthest south? ___English___

3. Where did most of the Africans settle? ___along the coast, to the east, by the water, in South Carolina and Virginia___

4. Which immigrant groups settled in all of the southern colonies?
English, Africans, Scotch-Irish

NAME _____ DATE _____

UNDERSTANDING PROVERBS IN *Poor Richard's Almanack*

Benjamin Franklin, a respected colonist, was and still is known for his political and scientific work. He was also a writer and printer who published a yearly almanac called *Poor Richard's Almanack.* Franklin's yearly almanacs were popular with the colonists because they contained a variety of features, including calendars, weather predictions, and recipes.

Analyze the Meaning of Proverbs

DIRECTIONS: Franklin also included proverbs in his almanac. A proverb is a short, commonly used saying that expresses a general truth. Below are some proverbs from Poor Richard's Almanack. Circle the statement below each proverb that best describes what the proverb means.

1. **Early to bed and early to rise makes a man healthy, wealthy, and wise.**

   (You will benefit from good habits and hard work.)

   You will be rich if you stick to your bedtime.

2. **Sell not virtue to purchase wealth, nor liberty to purchase power.**

   You will lose money if you try to buy wealth or power.

   (Do not sacrifice your values for money or power.)

3. **Don't throw stones at your neighbors, if your own windows are glass.**

   (Do not criticize others, because you have faults, too.)

   You can do what you want to others if you protect yourself first.

4. **Make haste slowly.**

   (Consider your actions carefully.)

   If you hurry, you can get more done.

5. **Tart words make no friends: a spoonful of honey will catch more flies than a gallon of vinegar.**

   (Speak kindly to others and you will have many friends.)

   You will make many friends if you feed them honey.

6. **Never leave that till tomorrow which you can do today.**

   (Get your work done today so you will not have more work tomorrow.)

   It's always better to leave work for the next day.

7. **No gains without pains.**

   Life is hard.

   (To get better at something, you must work hard at it.)

8. **Being ignorant is not so much a shame as being unwilling to learn.**

   (It is a waste not to be eager for an education.)

   People who are not smart are sad.

Events Leading to Revolution

Colonial printers turned out news sheets that often were hung in public places. These sheets told of events happening in the colonies.

Write Historical News Stories

DIRECTIONS: *Imagine you are writing a news sheet in the colonies. For each date below, write a headline for and a description of an important historical event.*

December 1773

Accept all answers that relate
to the Boston Tea Party.

April 18, 1775

Accept all answers that relate to the ride
of Paul Revere and William Dawes.

September 1774

Accept all answers that relate to the
First Continental Congress.

April 19, 1775

Accept all answers that relate to events
at Lexington and Concord.

Harcourt Brace School Publishers

HOW TO MAKE Economic Choices

Apply Critical Thinking Skills

DIRECTIONS: Imagine you have $20 to spend. Then complete the graphic organizer that follows to help you make an economic choice.

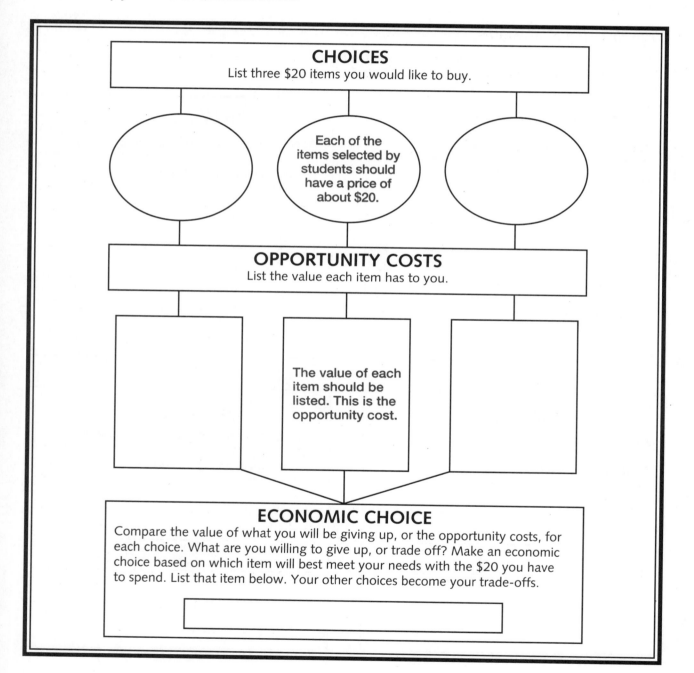

CHOICES
List three $20 items you would like to buy.

Each of the items selected by students should have a price of about $20.

OPPORTUNITY COSTS
List the value each item has to you.

The value of each item should be listed. This is the opportunity cost.

ECONOMIC CHOICE
Compare the value of what you will be giving up, or the opportunity costs, for each choice. What are you willing to give up, or trade off? Make an economic choice based on which item will best meet your needs with the $20 you have to spend. List that item below. Your other choices become your trade-offs.

Harcourt Brace School Publishers

Use after reading Chapter 7, Skill Lesson, page 285.

DIFFERENCES DIVIDE
Britain and Its Colonies

Connect Main Ideas

DIRECTIONS: Use this organizer to show how the chapter's main ideas are connected. Write three details to support each main idea.

Britain Rules the Colonies → **Differences Divide Britain and Its Colonies** → **Britain and the Colonies Go to War**

Government in the Colonies
The British colonists became unhappy with British rule.

1. Students' responses may include that the colonists could not vote,

2. had no representatives in Parliament, wanted to make their own laws,

3. and were angry that they weren't consulted about taxes.

Quarrels and Conflicts
Individuals and groups in the British colonies worked to make changes in their government.

1. Students should cite examples such as Mercy Otis Warren,

2. James Otis, Patrick Henry, Sons of Liberty, Daughters of Liberty,

3. Benjamin Franklin, and the Stamp Act Congress.

Colonists Unite
The colonists came together as they protested British rule.

1. Students should cite examples of unity, such as the Committees of

2. Correspondence, Boston Tea Party, Edenton Tea Party,

3. Continental Congress, formation of Minutemen fighters, and fighting at Lexington and Concord.

The Redcoats
ARE COMING!

Compare Visuals

DIRECTIONS: Compare the drawings of the Continental soldier's uniform and the British soldier's uniform. Then write C next to each statement below that describes a Continental uniform. Write B next to each statement that describes a British uniform. Write CB next to each statement that describes both uniforms.

Continental Uniform

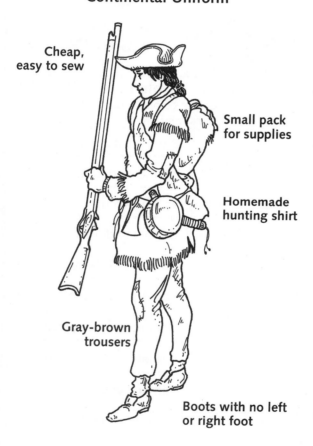

Cheap, easy to sew

Small pack for supplies

Homemade hunting shirt

Gray-brown trousers

Boots with no left or right foot

British Uniform

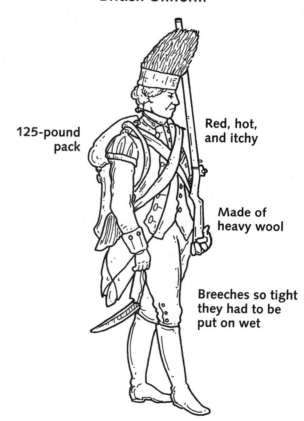

125-pound pack

Red, hot, and itchy

Made of heavy wool

Breeches so tight they had to be put on wet

B   hotter uniform

B   more visible in woods

CB   included a musket

CB   included a pack

C   more practical

C   included a canteen

B   knee-length boots

C   fringed shirt

C   three-cornered hat

C   included an ax

Use after reading Chapter 8, Lesson 1, pages 289–293.

NAME _____ DATE _____

HOW TO READ a Political Cartoon

Apply Reading and Research Skills

DIRECTIONS: France was an ally of the colonists during the
American Revolution. Examine the political cartoon below.
Then answer the questions that follow.

NOVEMBER 1780
French General, Count De Rochambeau, Reviewing the French Troops in America

1. When was this political cartoon drawn? November 1780

2. What conclusions can you draw about the cartoonist's opinion of the French soldiers?
The cartoonist had a very low opinion of the fighting ability of the French army.

3. What specific items in the cartoon led you to your conclusion?
backpacks shaped like large ear muffs, unflattering exaggeration of facial characteristics, emphasis

on ruffled shirts

Harcourt Brace School Publishers

A Woman Printed the Declaration of Independence

Only men drafted and signed the Declaration of Independence. Read the passage below to find out why Mary Katharine Goddard was chosen to print the Declaration of Independence.

Read Line by Line for Comprehension

DIRECTIONS: Use the line numbers in the passage to help you answer the questions that follow.

1   The Declaration of Independence was signed on July 4, 1776. By January 1777, it had
2 been printed seven times! There was, however, no official copy of the Declaration.
3 So, on January 18, 1777, Congress decided to print official copies for each state in
4 the new union.
5   The members of Congress wanted to find a local printer. This meant that they would
6 look in Baltimore, because that was where they were meeting. (By then, the British had
7 taken Philadelphia.) The logical choice was Mary Katharine Goddard.
8   Goddard was well known and experienced. She had a reputation for being a high-
9 quality printer. Goddard had learned the printing trade from her brother. She printed
10 her own newspaper, the *Maryland Journal,* and had even been the head of the post office of
11 Baltimore since 1775!
12   How can you tell the difference between the Declaration that Goddard printed and the other
13 copies? The one Goddard printed lists the delegates' names in neat columns next to the
14 states they represented. On the very bottom of the document, you will find "Baltimore,
15 In Maryland: Printed by Mary Katharine Goddard."

1. Which line tells you the number of times the Declaration had been printed by

January 1777? <u>line 2</u>

2. Which lines tell that Congress wanted to print official copies? <u>lines 2–4</u>

3. Lines 5–7 tell why the members of Congress wanted to find a printer in Baltimore.

What was their reason? <u>They were meeting in Baltimore and wanted a local printer.</u>

4. Reread lines 8–11. List the reasons Congress chose Goddard as the printer.

<u>Answers should include well known, experienced, high quality, good reputation.</u>

5. List the line numbers of the paragraph that explains how to tell the difference between the

Declaration that Goddard printed and the other copies. <u>lines 12–15</u>

Use after reading Chapter 8, Lesson 2, pages 295–299.

HOW TO LEARN FROM PICTURES

Apply Critical Thinking Skills

DIRECTIONS: By studying a picture carefully, you can learn a variety of information about a subject. Study the picture below of Patrick Henry speaking to The House of Burgesses against the Stamp Act. Then answer the questions that follow.

1. What part of the picture did you look at first? Why?

Accept answers that students can defend.

_____

_____

2. Are the people who are listening to Patrick Henry interested in what he is saying? How can you tell?

Acceptable answers should indicate that the audience is interested. Possible responses:

They are looking at Patrick Henry; they are listening to what he is saying.

_____

3. How do you think the people in the picture feel? How can you tell?

Possible responses might indicate that the people feel angry, worried, or upset.

Their facial expressions show this.

_____

_____

Harcourt Brace School Publishers

AMERICANS TAKE SIDES

Not all of the people living in the British colonies supported the fight for independence from Britain. About one third sided with the Loyalists, another third sided with the Patriots, and another third remained neutral.

Categorize Information

DIRECTIONS: *Write the following names or groups of people in the appropriate category in the chart below. You may wish to reread pages 301–305 in your textbook.*

Abigail Adams   Peter Salem
John Adams   Mary Slocumb
General Thomas Gage   Ethiopian Regiment
Patrick Henry   most Native Americans
Richard Henry Lee   many northern Anglicans
Peter Muhlenberg   many southern Presbyterians
John Murray   Quakers
Thomas Paine   Unmarried Ladies of America

LOYALIST	PATRIOT	NEUTRAL
General Thomas Gage	Abigail Adams	most Native Americans
John Murray	John Adams	Quakers
Ethiopian Regiment	Patrick Henry	
many northern Anglicans	Richard Henry Lee	
many southern Presbyterians	Peter Muhlenberg	
	Thomas Paine	
	Peter Salem	
	Mary Slocumb	
	Unmarried Ladies of America	

Use after reading Chapter 8, Lesson 3, pages 301–305.

Harcourt Brace School Publishers

Characterize Patriots

Map Characters in a Story

DIRECTIONS: Use the characters in Samuel's Choice to complete the organizer below. Describe each character's role by filling in the appropriate box.

SAMUEL ABRAHAM

main character of story,

14-year-old boy, slave,

worked for Loyalist

farmer, used owner's

boat to help Continental

army

SANA

Samuel's friend, a slave

who worked for same

Loyalist farmer as

Samuel, helped Samuel

with boat

THOMAS JEFFERSON

wrote "all men are

created equal" in the

Declaration of

Independence

SAMUEL'S CHOICE

ISAAC VAN DITMAS

Loyalist farmer and slave

owner, owned Samuel and

Sana, arrested for helping

British, exchanged property

(including Samuel and

Sana) for freedom

TOBY AND NATHANIEL

slave friends of Samuel

and Sana

MORDECAI GIST

commissioned Samuel

to use boat to help

Continental army

GEORGE WASHINGTON

leader of Continental

army

Which Event Happened First?

Sequence Events

DIRECTIONS: In each pair of events of the American Revolution, circle the event that happened first.

1.	(Committees of Correspondence formed)	Second Continental Congress formed
2.	Second Continental Congress formed	(Battle of Lexington and Concord)
3.	(Second Continental Congress formed)	Olive Branch Petition sent to King George III
4.	Winter at Valley Forge	(Battle of Bunker Hill)
5.	Richard Henry Lee gives speech to Second Continental Congress declaring free and independent states	(Thomas Paine's *Common Sense* published)
6.	Jefferson plans the Declaration	(Second Continental Congress formed)
7.	George Washington's troops almost wiped out after winter at Valley Forge	(Declaration of Independence signed)
8.	(Colonists' victory at Saratoga)	French join Revolution on colonists' side
9.	Treaty of Paris signed in 1783	(Battle of Yorktown)
10.	Treaty of Paris signed in 1783	(Benedict Arnold becomes a traitor)

Use after reading Chapter 8, Lesson 5, pages 310–317.

The War for Independence

Connect Main Ideas

DIRECTIONS: Use this organizer to show how the chapter's main ideas are connected. Write the main idea of each lesson.

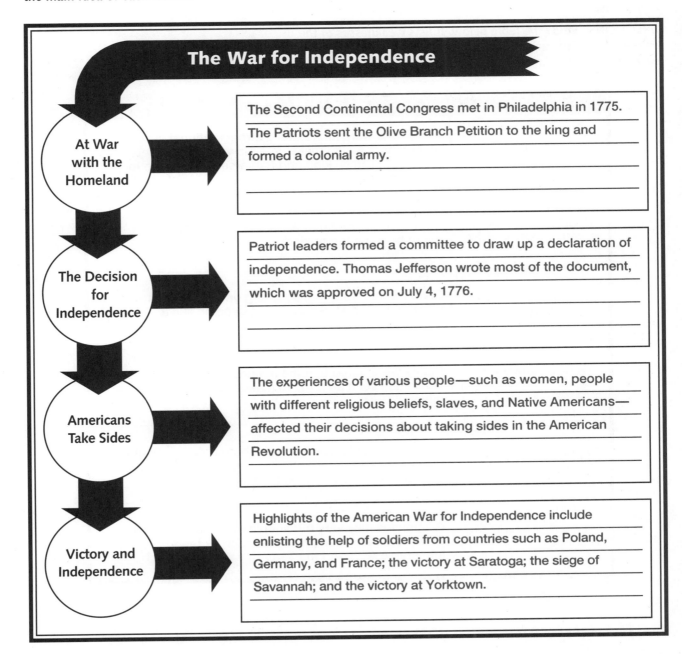

The War for Independence

At War with the Homeland
→ The Second Continental Congress met in Philadelphia in 1775. The Patriots sent the Olive Branch Petition to the king and formed a colonial army.

The Decision for Independence
→ Patriot leaders formed a committee to draw up a declaration of independence. Thomas Jefferson wrote most of the document, which was approved on July 4, 1776.

Americans Take Sides
→ The experiences of various people—such as women, people with different religious beliefs, slaves, and Native Americans—affected their decisions about taking sides in the American Revolution.

Victory and Independence
→ Highlights of the American War for Independence include enlisting the help of soldiers from countries such as Poland, Germany, and France; the victory at Saratoga; the siege of Savannah; and the victory at Yorktown.

Articles of Confederation

The Articles of Confederation united 13 independent states. The Articles gave the national government certain powers, but because Americans wanted to guard their newly won freedom, the national government they formed was weak.

Identify Reasons

DIRECTIONS: Study the table below. It lists weaknesses of the Articles of Confederation. Complete the table by filling in a reason for each weakness.

WEAKNESS	REASON
There was no strong national government.	Americans were afraid that a strong national government would make unfair laws for the states, just as the British king and Parliament had made for the colonies.
At least 9 of the 13 states had to agree on any law or decision.	States were afraid that a small group of states might become too powerful.
No single leader controlled the government.	States were afraid that by giving one person too much power, that person might become like a monarch.
Congress could not raise a national army without the permission of the states.	States were afraid that the national government would use such an army to make them obey national laws.
Congress could not collect taxes.	Accept all reasonable answers, but students should make reference to "taxation without representation" as experienced by colonists under British rule.
Congress could not make laws about trade.	Responses may vary but should make reference to Britain's unfair trade practices, such as the Intolerable Acts and the Tea Act.

Harcourt Brace School Publishers

Use after reading Chapter 9, Lesson 1, pages 333–337.

Who Was There?

Identify Historical Figures

DIRECTIONS: From the list at the right, choose the person who might be describing his part in the Constitutional Convention. Write the letter identifying his name in the correct blank below.

A. John Adams
B. Patrick Henry
C. John Hancock
D. Thomas Jefferson
E. Daniel Shays
F. Benjamin Franklin
G. James Madison
H. Gouverneur Morris
I. George Washington
J. Samuel Adams

_G_ **1.** In 1779 I was elected to represent Virginia as a member of Congress under the Articles of Confederation.

_I_ **2.** I was elected president of the Constitutional Convention.

_J_ **3.** I was sick, so I could not attend the Constitutional Convention.

_B_ **4.** I refused to take part in the Constitutional Convention because I did not believe that a stronger national government was a good idea.

_D_ **5.** I said of the Constitutional Convention, "It really is an assembly of demigods."

_G_ **6.** I was Congress's youngest member at 29 years of age.

_F_ **7.** I was carried to the Constitutional Convention in a Chinese sedan chair.

_D_ **8.** I could not attend the Constitutional Convention because I was in Paris as the United States ambassador to France.

_H_ **9.** I changed the opening words in the Preamble to the Constitution to read, "We the people of the United States. . . ."

_A_ **10.** I could not attend the Constitutional Convention because I was in London as the United States ambassador to Britain.

_C_ **11.** I was too busy as governor of Massachusetts to attend the convention.

_E_ **12.** As a frontier farmer, I was not invited to the convention.

_H_ **13.** I was given the job of writing down all the ideas that were approved during the convention.

_I_ **14.** I was the most honored hero of the American Revolution.

Harcourt Brace School Publishers

HOW TO FIGURE TRAVEL TIME AND DISTANCE

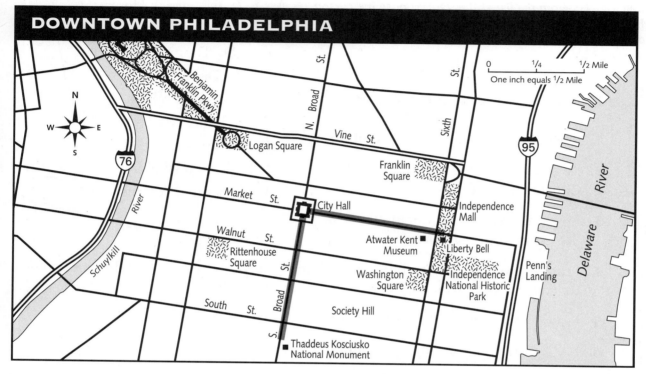

DOWNTOWN PHILADELPHIA

 Apply Map and Globe Skills

DIRECTIONS: Study the map above to complete the following activities.

1. Draw the following route on the map: You are at the Liberty Bell. Go west on Market Street to City Hall. Head south on S. Broad Street to Thaddeus Kosciusko National Monument.

2. On this map, 1 inch stands for ½ mile. Use a ruler to measure the number of inches covered by the route you drew. Write your answer here. ___3 inches___

3. Multiply the total number of inches traveled by ½ (the number of miles equal to 1 inch). This will tell you the total number of miles that would be traveled if you walked this route in Philadelphia. ___3 × ½ = 1½ miles___

4. To find out how long it would take to travel this route at different speeds, divide the total number of miles by the rate of travel shown below.

Walking (3 mph): ___1½ ÷ 3 = ½ hour (30 minutes)___

Jogging (6 mph): ___1½ ÷ 6 = ¼ hour (15 minutes)___

Use after reading Chapter 9, Skill Lesson, pages 344–345.

Harcourt Brace School Publishers

Who Has the Power?

Compare Government Systems

DIRECTIONS: Use the diagram on page 347 of your textbook and the information from Chapter 9 to complete the following activities. Put an N next to powers that belong to the national government, an S next to powers that belong to state governments, and a B next to powers that are shared by both.

<u>B</u> **1.** (Raise money by taxing citizens)

<u>S</u> **2.** Set up public schools

<u>S</u> **3.** Set rules for state and local elections

<u>N</u> **4.** Print and coin money ✔

<u>N</u> **5.** (Raise an army and a navy)

<u>N</u> **6.** (Make laws for immigration)

<u>N</u> **7.** (Control trade among states)

<u>S</u> **8.** Control trade within states

<u>B</u> **9.** (Set up courts)

<u>N</u> **10.** Declare war ✔

<u>N</u> **11.** Admit new states ✔

<u>S</u> **12.** Make laws for marriage and divorce

DIRECTIONS: Compare the powers granted to the national government by the Constitution with those granted to it by the Articles of Confederation. Use the information above to complete the activities that follow. You may need to review Lesson 1 on the Articles of Confederation.

1. Put a check mark next to those powers of the national government that are the same under the Constitution as they were under the Articles of Confederation.

2. Circle the powers of the national government that are new under the Constitution.

3. Think about what your life might be like if the Articles of Confederation still governed the United States. Then use information summarized in the activities on this page to write a paragraph that explains why the Constitution made the United States a stronger country.

Answers may vary but should include references to the power to raise money by taxing citizens, to

raise an army and a navy, to control trade among states, and to set up courts.

_____

_____

_____

HOW TO COMPROMISE TO RESOLVE CONFLICTS

Apply Participation Skills

DIRECTIONS: Complete the graphic organizer that follows. For each step, write in the arguments, decisions, or both made at the Constitutional Convention that led to the Great Compromise.

BOTH SIDES CLEARLY STATE WANTS AND NEEDS

Accept all answers that consider the interests of large states versus those of small states; large states wanted representation by population (Virginia Plan), and small states wanted one vote per state (New Jersey Plan).

BOTH SIDES UNDERSTAND WHAT IS TO BE GIVEN UP

Accept all answers that indicate students understand that each group may need to give up some power and representation.

BOTH SIDES DECIDE WHAT IS MOST IMPORTANT

Answers may include that each side has some things that it is not willing to give up—such as preventing the other side from having too much power or representation.

BOTH SIDES DISCUSS POSSIBLE COMPROMISES

Answers may make reference to Washington's setting up a committee of one representative from each state to work out a compromise; the realization that without compromise, there would be no government; Sherman's plan; or the new compromise about tax bills.

BOTH SIDES VOTE ON COMPROMISES

Answers should mention the committee's compromise and then the presentation to the whole convention of the Great Compromise.

Harcourt Brace School Publishers

Use after reading Chapter 9, Skill Lesson, page 352.

Who Does What in
THE GOVERNMENT?

Diagram the United States Government

DIRECTIONS: Study the diagram on page 354 of your textbook that shows how a bill becomes a law. Then order the steps of the process below from 1 to 6.

_6_ The bill becomes a law or is sent back to Congress for another vote.

_1_ A member of the House or the Senate introduces a bill.

_4_ The President reviews the bill.

_2_ Congressional committees review the bill.

_5_ The President either vetoes the bill or signs it into law.

_3_ Both houses of Congress vote to approve the bill.

DIRECTIONS: Study the diagram on page 356 of your textbook that shows how checks and balances work. Then complete the chart below by writing in the branch that holds each particular power and the branch being checked. The first one has been completed for you.

BRANCH HOLDING AUTHORITY	CHECK/BALANCE	BRANCH BEING CHECKED
Legislative	Override the President's veto	Executive
Executive	Appoint Supreme Court justices	Judicial
Judicial	Rule President's actions unconstitutional	Executive
Executive	Veto a bill	Legislative
Legislative	Approve treaties	Executive
Legislative	Approve appointments of Supreme Court justices	Executive

Harcourt Brace School Publishers

Constitutional Footnotes

Understand a Primary Source

DIRECTIONS: Read the Preamble to the United States Constitution below. Then figure out what the footnoted, or numbered, words and phrases mean. Write the number of the footnote next to the best explanation.

We the people of the United States,
in order to form a more perfect Union,[1]
establish justice,[2]
insure domestic tranquillity,[3]
provide for the common defense,[4]
promote the general welfare,[5] and
secure the blessings of liberty[6]
to ourselves[7]
and our posterity,[8]
do ordain[9]
and establish[10]
this Constitution for the United States of America.

_____2_____ **a.** set up a fair system

_____10_____ **b.** set up

_____3_____ **c.** make sure there is peace at home

_____1_____ **d.** make a better government

_____9_____ **e.** make official

_____4_____ **f.** supply protection for all

_____5_____ **g.** encourage health, happiness, and comfort

_____6_____ **h.** gain and keep the gifts of freedom

_____8_____ **i.** everyone who later becomes part of this country

_____7_____ **j.** everyone belonging to this country

Use after reading Chapter 9, Lesson 5, pages 358–363.

The Constitution

Connect Main Ideas

DIRECTIONS: Use this organizer to show how the chapter's main ideas are connected. Write the main idea of each lesson, and list the three branches of government.

The Constitution

The Articles of Confederation
The Articles of Confederation had strengths and weaknesses, such as allowing Congress to decide how to divide and govern western lands and set laws by which new states would be formed but not allowing it to raise an army, make laws about trade or taxes, or establish a national court.

A New Plan of Government
The Constitution would create a better plan of government, work toward justice and peace, promote the country's well-being, allow the nation to defend itself against enemies, and provide liberty for its citizens.

Debates and Compromises
Debates and compromises at the Constitutional Convention revolved around such issues as the relationship between states and the new national government, how states would be represented in the legislature, how much each state should pay to support the government, and the future of slavery.

The legislative branch would make the laws.

The executive branch would carry out the laws.

The judicial branch would settle differences about the meaning of the laws.

A Government of Three Branches
Three branches of government would create a separation of powers.

Use after reading Chapter 9, pages 332–365.

The MAZE of RATIFICATION

Sequence States

DIRECTIONS: *Use the map and the table on page 369 of your textbook to get through the maze of ratification. Draw a line from Start to the first state to ratify the Constitution. Then continue through the maze to connect the remaining states in the order of their ratification.*

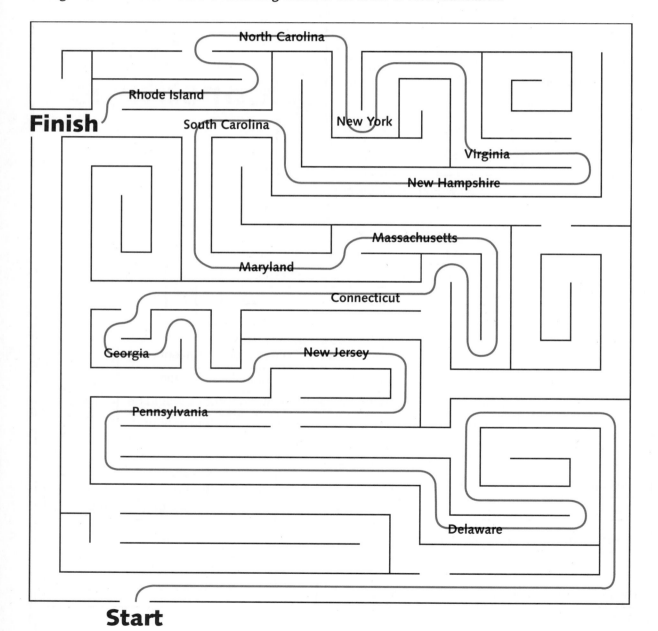

Use after reading Chapter 10, Lesson 1, pages 367–371.

Counting the Amendments

Number the Bill of Rights

DIRECTIONS: Read the list of freedoms below, and decide which amendment protects each one. Write the amendment's number in the box opposite each freedom. If all your answers are correct, you can add the numbers in each of the three columns and one of your totals will equal the number of amendments in the Bill of Rights. Circle the correct total.

1. Right to "keep and bear arms"

2. Right to a speedy and public trial

3. Freedom of speech

4. Freedom to hold meetings and to ask the government to hear complaints

5. Freedom from being forced to quarter soldiers

6. Protection of rights that are not listed in the Constitution

7. Freedom of religion

8. Protection against the national government's doing things not listed in the Constitution

9. Freedom of the press

10. Protection against the government's ordering an unreasonable search of a home

**TOTAL NUMBER OF AMENDMENTS
IN BILL OF RIGHTS**

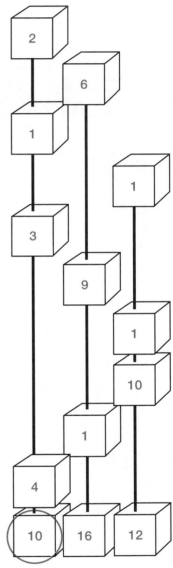

Who's in Office?

Organize Information

DIRECTIONS: Complete the following graphic organizer about the first United States government under the Constitution. Use the information in your textbook as a guide.

THE FIRST U.S. GOVERNMENT

EXECUTIVE BRANCH

President

George Washington

Vice President

John Adams

CABINET

Secretary of	State	was	Thomas Jefferson
Secretary of	Treasury	was	Alexander Hamilton
Secretary of	War	was	Henry Knox
Attorney	General	was	Edmund Randolph

LEGISLATIVE BRANCH

The two houses

House of Representatives

Senate

JUDICIAL BRANCH

Chief Justice

John Jay

Use after reading Chapter 10, Lesson 3, pages 378–384.

HOW TO LEARN FROM A DOCUMENT

This résumé, or summary of experience, lists information Benjamin Banneker might have written about himself. The cover of Banneker's almanac lists information about his publication.

Résumé
BENJAMIN BANNEKER

- Born in Baltimore, Maryland, 1731

- Son of free Africans

- Learned to read from grandmother

- Self-taught in mathematics and astronomy

- Talented in mechanical sciences

- Made first wooden clock in America

- First important African scientist in the United States

- Served for two years on the commission to survey and plan the city of Washington, D.C.

- Wrote and published annual almanac with at least 29 editions

Apply Reading and Research Skills

DIRECTIONS: Study the two documents above. Then complete the activities that follow.

1. Underline the title of Banneker's publication.

2. Circle the year in which Banneker's work was published.

3. Put a star next to the city in which Banneker's work was printed.

4. What do you think is Banneker's most interesting accomplishment? Explain why.

Answers should reflect students' personal choices, but students should substantiate their choices

and point out the obstacles that Banneker had to overcome.

Harcourt Brace School Publishers

A New Government Begins

Connect Main Ideas

DIRECTIONS: Use this organizer to show how the chapter's main ideas are connected. Write a sentence or two describing how each idea shown below helped to build a new government.

A New Government Begins

Approving the Constitution

The new Constitution gained support once a promise was made to add a bill of rights to the Constitution after it was ratified.

Rights and Responsibilities

Citizens' responsibilities and rights come from the Constitution. In the Bill of Rights, the Constitution describes the freedoms that government cannot take away and lists the actions that the government is not allowed to take. The Constitution implies that citizens should respect and obey the law, vote, defend the country, serve on juries, and pay taxes.

Putting the New Government to Work

The country's early leaders compromised to make the Constitution and the government work. They set up ties with leading world powers, set up a new banking system, passed new tax laws, built an army, and worked together in the President's Cabinet.

Harcourt Brace School Publishers

Use after reading Chapter 10, pages 366–387.

BLAZING A TRAIL WEST

Identify Historical Figures

DIRECTIONS: On the blanks provided, write the word or name that best completes each sentence. Some letters in your answers will have numbers under them. Write these letters in the appropriate boxes below, and you will find the name of Daniel Boone's wife.

1. After the Revolutionary War, the land between the Appalachian Mountains and the Mississippi River was called the American F R O N T I E R .

(1 under R)

2. Settlers west of the Appalachians were called P I O N E E R S .

(12 under O)

3. Daniel Boone came to love the woods and hunting after his family moved to the Y A D K I N   V A L L E Y of North Carolina.

(10 under Y, 11 under V)

4. A man named J O H N   F I N L E Y told Boone stories about land far to the west over the Appalachian Mountains.

(4 under E)

5. After the French and Indian War, Boone set out to find an Indian trail called the W A R R I O R ' S   P A T H .

(9 under R)

6. Boone told about the rich land and buffalo in K E N T U C K Y .

(6 under C)

7. Both the C H E R O K E E S and Shawnees lived in settlements throughout Kentucky.

(5 under C, 2 under E)

8. Boone cleared a path through the Cumberland Gap that came to be known as the W I L D E R N E S S   R O A D .

(7 under A)

9. Boone built a fort in this wilderness and named the new pioneer settlement B O O N E S B O R O U G H .

(8 under B, 3 under E)

R	E	B	E	C	C	A		B	R	Y	A	N
1	2	3	4	5	6	7		8	9	10	11	12

Harcourt Brace School Publishers

Follow their Footsteps

Identify Historical Figures

DIRECTIONS: Each of the footprints below contains a paragraph that could have been written by one of the people involved with the Lewis and Clark expedition. Write the name of that person in the space provided.

One of my greatest accomplishments was the Louisiana Purchase. I asked the members of the Corps of Discovery to learn all they could about this new land.

Thomas
_____
Jefferson
_____

As chief of the Shoshones, I welcomed the members of the Corps of Discovery. I was especially happy to see my sister. To help Lewis and Clark make their way over the Rockies, I gave them horses.

Chief
_____
Cameahwait
_____

I was William Clark's slave. My skills in hunting and fishing made a valuable contribution to this exciting and informative expedition.

York
_____
_____

The leader of the expedition was my good friend. He chose me to go on the expedition because of my skills in cartography. We called our group of explorers the Corps of Discovery.

William Clark
_____
_____

I was a Shoshone. The members of the expedition asked me to go with them to translate when they reached my tribe's lands. I agreed to go.

Sacagawea
_____
_____

After working as an army officer in the wilderness of the Northwest Territory, I led the expedition to explore the lands of the Louisiana Purchase. I kept a journal of our experiences.

Meriwether Lewis
_____
_____

Use after reading Chapter 11, Lesson 2, pages 408–413.

Harcourt Brace School Publishers

The Growth of NATIONALISM

Understand Cause and Effect

DIRECTIONS: Complete the following chart. Fill in either the cause or the effect.

Accept all reasonable answers. Use the following completed chart as a guide.

CAUSES	EFFECTS
Harrison sends 1,000 soldiers to Prophetstown, _____ the Shawnee headquarters. Tenskwatawa orders the Indians to attack first.	The Americans and the Indians fight in the Battle of Tippecanoe.
Many people in the Northwest Territory blame _____ Britain for Indian attacks. People in the South are angry about _____ impressment of American sailors _____ and stopping of trade. War Hawks are eager for more land. _____	War fever pushes Congress to declare war on Britain in 1812.
American Captain Oliver Hazard Perry defeats the British in a battle on Lake Erie on September 10, 1813.	British control on the Great Lakes is weakened. Harrison moves soldiers into Canada. _____
The War of 1812 ends. _____	A wave of nationalism sweeps the country.
President Monroe wants to stop the growth of Spanish, French, and British colonies in the Americas.	President Monroe announces the Monroe _____ Doctrine.

HOW TO PREDICT A LIKELY OUTCOME

Apply Critical Thinking Skills

DIRECTIONS: The following flow chart lists the steps for predicting likely outcomes. Choose a school event, such as a test, that you expect to happen soon. Copy the flow chart onto another sheet of paper and use the steps to predict the outcome of the event.

Accept all reasonable predictions that students can substantiate.

THINK ABOUT WHAT YOU KNOW.

MAKE A PREDICTION.

READ OR GATHER MORE INFORMATION.

ASK YOURSELF SOME QUESTIONS:

Does the new information support my prediction?

Do I need to change my prediction?

DECIDE IF YOUR PREDICTION SEEMS CORRECT.

GO THROUGH THE STEPS AGAIN, IF NECESSARY.

Harcourt Brace School Publishers

Use after reading Chapter 11, Skill Lesson, page 421.

The Flag
was still there

After the British attack on Fort McHenry, Francis Scott Key peered through the early dawn and saw that the American flag still flew over the fort. He wrote the words to "The Star-Spangled Banner," our national anthem, to honor this national symbol.

Understand Patriotic Symbols

DIRECTIONS: Read the statements below. Decide which statements tell how to respect and care for the flag and which statements give general information about the flag. Then place an X in the appropriate column.

THE FLAG	RESPECT/CARE	GENERAL INFORMATION
1. The present flag has 64 separate elements.		X
2. The flag has the exact shades of blue and red, which are numbers 70075 and 70180 in the *Standard Color Card of America.*		X
3. The flag is to be flown at half-mast as a mark of respect after the death of a major official.	X	
4. The present flag dates back to July 4, 1960, when the fiftieth star was added for Hawaii.		X
5. The flag is taken down in bad weather.	X	
6. The flag is never to be allowed to touch anything beneath it, such as the ground, the floor, or water.	X	
7. The United States flag is called the "Stars and Stripes."		X
8. The flag that Key wrote about had 15 stars and 15 stripes.		X
9. Congress passed a law in 1818 requiring the flag to have 13 stripes to represent the original 13 colonies.		X
10. The flag is to be displayed during school days in or near every school.	X	

Harcourt Brace School Publishers

Use after reading Chapter 11, Lesson 4, pages 422–427.

ON THE MOVE

Connect Main Ideas

DIRECTIONS: Use this organizer to show how the chapter's main ideas are connected. Write one or two sentences to tell about each person or pair of people or to summarize each event or idea.

On the Move

Across the Appalachians

Daniel Boone A pioneer who helped settle Kentucky, Boone traveled through the Cumberland Gap.

Settling Kentucky The United States gained Kentucky when the Virginia militia defeated the Indians. Boone cleared the Wilderness Road for pioneers to get to the new territory and built the first settlement, named Boonesborough.

Pioneer Life Leading difficult lives, pioneers had to clear their land, build their homes, grow their food, and make their own clothes and tools.

The Louisiana Purchase

The Purchase The Louisiana territory—sold to the United States by Napoleon Bonaparte for $15 million—doubled the size of the country.

Lewis and Clark Led an expedition that mapped out major rivers and mountains to help pioneers find their way from St. Louis to the Pacific Coast.

Zebulon Pike Led an expedition to explore the southwestern part of the Louisiana Purchase.

A Second War with Britain

Tecumseh and the Prophet Shawnee Indians who wanted to form a confederation with other tribes to unite against the American pioneers.

The War of 1812 Due to anger at the British for their interference in trade, Congress voted to declare war on Britain in 1812.

The Era of Good Feelings From 1815–1824, nationalism united the people of the United States, creating a feeling of pride in the country.

Use after reading Chapter 11, pages 402–429.

Harcourt Brace School Publishers

Inventors and their Inventions

Link Past Technology to the Present

DIRECTIONS: Complete the following chart about inventions of the Industrial Revolution by filling in the missing information.

INVENTOR	INVENTION	IMPORTANCE OF INVENTION	WHAT YOUR LIFE WOULD BE LIKE WITHOUT THE INVENTION
Unknown	spinning machine	made large textile mills possible; brought the Industrial Revolution to the United States	Answers in this column should reflect students' understanding of uses of these inventions.
Eli Whitney	interchangeable parts	mass production	
Francis Cabot Lowell	one-factory system	workers with different skills working under one roof	
Robert Fulton	steamboat, the *Clermont*	speeded travel and trade over water	
Peter Cooper	locomotive, the *Tom Thumb*	speeded travel and trade over land	

Harcourt Brace School Publishers

Use after reading Chapter 12, Lesson 1, pages 431–438.

The Trail of Tears

Sequence Events

DIRECTIONS: Read the following events leading up to the Trail of Tears. Then identify the year in which each event took place. You may wish to review the information in your textbook before you begin.

_____1829_____ Gold is discovered on Cherokee lands; settlers pour in to stake their claims.

_____1832_____ Chief Justice John Marshall gives the Court's ruling that the United States should protect the Cherokees and their lands in Georgia, but President Jackson ignores the ruling.

____(1830)____ Congress passes the Indian Removal Act, forcing all Indians living east of the Mississippi to move to the Indian Territory.

_____1791_____ The United States government agrees to accept the independence of the Cherokee nation.

_____1829_____ Andrew Jackson becomes the seventh President of the United States.

_____1838_____ A large group of Cherokees begin the journey that has come to be known as the Trail of Tears; more than 4,000 Cherokees die.

DIRECTIONS: Use the information above to complete the following activities.

1. Circle the date of the event that marks the beginning of forced relocation of native peoples from the East to the West.

2. Underline an economic reason why the Cherokees were forced from their lands.

3. Draw a box around the year that marks the beginning of the Trail of Tears.

4. On a separate sheet of paper, draw a horizontal time line using the dates and events listed above. Start your time line at 1790 and end it at 1840. Make one inch represent a ten-year period.

Accept all time lines with the following characteristics: all dates and events listed in the correct order, starts at 1790 with ten-year increments every inch up to 1840, and measures 5" in length.

Use after reading Chapter 12, Lesson 2, pages 439–443.

Harcourt Brace School Publishers

THE Oregon Trail

Arrange Information in Order

DIRECTIONS: Read the following sentences about a trip on the Oregon Trail. Then place the sentences in the proper order by numbering them from 1 to 6, with 1 being the earliest event and 6 being the latest event.

___2___ A steamboat carries our family up the river from St. Louis to Independence, Missouri.

___6___ The wagons in our group finally arrive in Willamette Valley. Oregon at last!

___4___ At nightfall the wagons in our group circle for camp.

___3___ In Independence we load our possessions onto a wagon and hear the cry, "Wagons roll!"

___1___ We leave our home in the East and board a train headed for St. Louis, Missouri.

___5___ In the morning we eat breakfast, and then continue our journey by wagon to Oregon.

DIRECTIONS: Study the list of supplies below. Then complete the activities that follow.

One box of sardines	$16	_1_
One pound of hard bread	$ 2	_4_
One pound of butter	$ 6	_2_
One-half pound of cheese	$ 3	_3_
Total	$27	

1. Number the items from most expensive to least expensive in the spaces provided. Start numbering with *1* as the most expensive.

2. Write the total cost of the supplies in the space provided.

3. Imagine that you can spend only $25. Put a line through the item or items that you would have to take off your list. Answers will vary, although many students may put a line through "one pound of hard bread," which costs $2.

Harcourt Brace School Publishers

NAME _____ DATE _____

HOW TO USE RELIEF and Elevation Maps

Map Skill *Apply Map and Globe Skills*

DIRECTIONS: Study the map of the Oregon Trail.
Then answer the questions that follow.

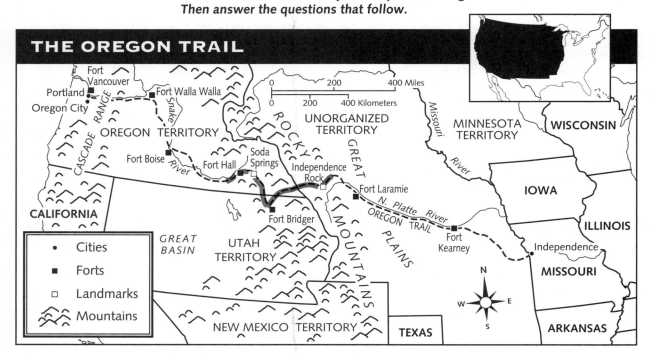

THE OREGON TRAIL

1. Write in the correct sequence the names of the physical features you would pass through
   if you traveled the Oregon Trail from Independence, Missouri, to Fort Vancouver.

   Great Plains, N. Platte River, Rocky Mountains, Snake River, Cascade Range

   _____

   _____

2. Trace over the part of the Oregon Trail that passes through the Rocky Mountains.

   Through which forts does this part of the trail pass? Fort Bridger and Fort Hall

3. Which river did the Oregon Trail follow just west of the Rocky Mountains?

   Snake River

4. On a separate sheet of paper, describe the trip along the Oregon Trail from
   Independence to Portland. Include in your description the forts and landmarks
   along the way and the changes in the geography.   Answers may vary but should include
   descriptions of forts and landmarks as well as of plains and mountainous areas.

Use after reading Chapter 12, Skill Lesson, pages 452–453.

Harcourt Brace School Publishers

Seneca Falls

Compare Primary Sources

DIRECTIONS: Read the following opening lines of the Declaration of Sentiments by Elizabeth Cady Stanton. Complete the activities that follow by comparing these lines with the opening lines of the Declaration of Independence which can be found on page R19 in your textbook.

Declaration of Sentiments

When, in the course of human events, it becomes necessary for one portion of the family of man to assume among the people of the earth a position different from that which they have hitherto occupied, but one to which the laws of nature and of nature's God entitle them, a decent respect to the opinions of mankind requires that they should declare the causes that impel them to such a course.

We hold these truths to be self-evident: that all men and women are created equal; that they are endowed by their Creator with certain inalienable rights; that among these are life, liberty, and the pursuit of happiness. . . .

1. Underline the words in the Declaration of Sentiments that are different from the words in the Declaration of Independence.

2. Why do you think the author of this document did not change the word "mankind"?

Accept answers that discuss the historical usage of the word *mankind*, which was used at that time

to refer to both men and women.

3. Write the phrase from the Declaration of Independence that was completely left out of the Declaration of Sentiments. (Don't include words used as substitutes.)

to dissolve the political bands which have connected them with another

4. Why do you think the author would model the Declaration of Sentiments after the Declaration of Independence?

Accept answers that refer to the Declaration of Independence, which expresses the rights of the

people, as a document Americans respect.

HOW TO USE A
Double-Bar Graph

Apply Chart and Graph Skills

DIRECTIONS: Use the facts at the right to make a double-bar graph in the space below. Create a key and title for your graph. Then answer the questions on the next page.

KEY

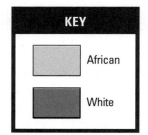

African

White

POPULATION GROWTH 1790–1860 (IN THOUSANDS)		
YEAR	**AFRICAN**	**WHITE**
1790	757	3,172
1800	1,002	4,306
1810	1,378	5,862
1820	1,772	7,867
1830	2,329	10,537
1840	2,874	14,196
1850	3,639	19,553
1860	4,442	26,923

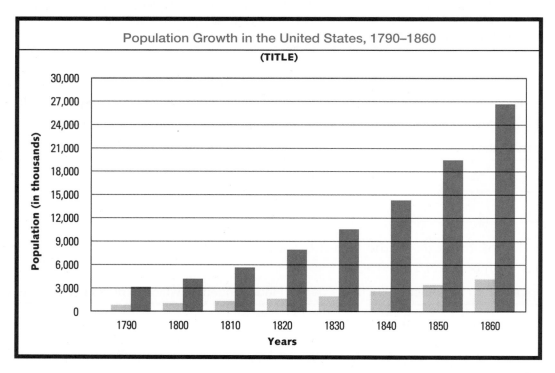

Population Growth in the United States, 1790–1860
(TITLE)

(continued)

Use after reading Chapter 12, Skill Lesson, page 459.

Harcourt Brace School Publishers

1. What interval is used on the bar graph to show the increase in population?
   Accept either 3,000 or 3,000,000.

2. What interval is used to show the passage of time? __10 years__

3. How many years of data does this bar graph cover? __70 years__

4. During which ten-year period did the white population grow the least?
   1790–1800

5. During which ten-year period was there the least growth in the African population?
   1790–1800

6. Compare the growth of the African population with that of the white population.
   List two generalizations you can make using the data.
   Answers include: white population grew more but also started with a larger population; both African
   and white populations grew steadily, but white population grew faster; white population is always
   larger than African population regardless of growth.

7. Compare the table on page 82 with the double-bar graph you created. Which of the
   two makes it easier for you to understand the information? Why?
   Accept all answers that students can defend.

THE WAY WEST

Connect Main Ideas

DIRECTIONS: Use this organizer to show how the chapter's main ideas are connected. Write three details to support each main idea.

The Industrial Revolution
New technology changed life in the United States in the 1800s.

1. Textile technology brought to the United States in 1790.

2. Manufacturing became more efficient when spinning, dyeing, and weaving were combined.

3. Advances in transportation, such as the Erie Canal, National Road, and railroads, spurred the Industrial Revolution.

The Age of Jackson
Problems divided the American people in the early 1800s.

1. Sectionalism led to long debates over states' versus the Union's rights.

2. South Carolina threatened to secede because of tariffs.

3. President Jackson forced Cherokees to move to the Indian Territory.

The Way West W — E

N

S

Westward Ho!
The United States expanded its territory in the 1800s.

1. A treaty is signed with Britain to establish the United States-Canadian border and acquire Oregon, Washington, Idaho, Wyoming, and western Montana.

2. By acquiring California, the United States would be able to build ports on the Pacific Ocean.

3. The Treaty of Guadalupe Hidalgo forced Mexico to give the United States California, Arizona, New Mexico, and Utah.

An Age of Reform
People in the 1800s worked to make American society better.

1. Educational reforms improved public schools.

2. Abolitionists worked to end slavery.

3. Reformers worked to gain rights for women, including the right to vote.

Harcourt Brace School Publishers

NAME _____ DATE _____

A TALE OF TWO REGIONS
1860

Analyze Information in a Table

DIRECTIONS: The table below compares the North with the South in 1860. Use the information in your textbook to complete the table. Then answer the questions that follow to show that you understand how the two regions differed.

TWO WAYS OF LIFE: 1860		
	NORTH	**SOUTH**
Total Number of People	More than 19 million	About 11 million
Number of Enslaved People	– 0 –	Nearly 4 million
Number of Factories	119,500	20,850
Number of Factory Workers	1,300,000	110,000
Annual Value of Factory Products	$1,730,000,000	$156,000,000
Miles of Railroad Track	21,500	8,500
Value of Exports	$175,000,000	$226,000,000
Money in Banks	$345,900,000	$76,000,000

1. List three details from the table that support the idea that there was more manufacturing in the North than in the South.

The North had more factories than the South.

The North had more factory workers than the South.

The annual value of factory products was greater in the North than in the South.

2. List one detail from the table that supports the idea that the South relied on trade with other countries more than the North did. The value of exports from the South was greater than the value of exports from the North.

3. Which region had more miles of railroad track? the North
How might having more miles of railroad track affect that region's economy?

Responses will vary but should reflect an understanding that having more miles of railroad track might lead to increased profits from trade.

Use after reading Chapter 13, Lesson 1, pages 477–482.

HOW TO USE Graphs To Identify Trends

In the early 1800s most people in both the North and the South lived and worked on farms. Today, farming continues to be an important economic activity throughout much of the United States. However, the number of farms has changed greatly over time.

Apply Chart and Graph Skills

DIRECTIONS: Use the facts at the right to make a line graph in the space below. Add a title to your graph. Then answer the questions that follow.

Year	Number of Farms
1850	1,500,000
1880	4,000,000
1920	6,500,000
1980	2,400,000
1992	2,100,000

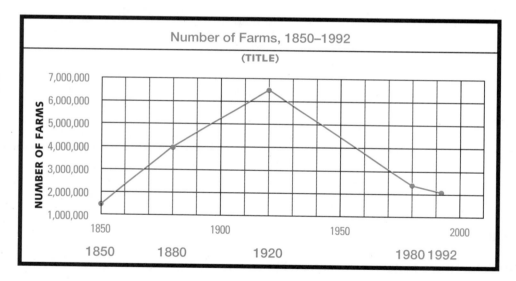

1. What was the trend between 1850 and 1920? The number of farms increased.

2. What was the trend between 1920 and 1992? The number of farms decreased.

3. How would you explain the trends? Possible responses: increases in population from 1850 to 1920 led to an increase in the number of farms; technology has made farms more productive, so fewer farms are needed today; modern machinery allows larger farms, reducing the total number of farms; fewer people choose to live on farms today.

Use after reading Chapter 13, Skill Lesson, page 483.

THE LIFE AND TIMES OF A
SLAVE

Gather Information in Reference Books

DIRECTIONS: Read the passage from Frederick Douglass's autobiography, The Life and Times of Frederick Douglass.

My first experience of life, as I now remember it, began in the family of my grandmother and grandfather, Betsey and Isaac Bailey. . . .

. . . Whether because she [Grandmother Betsey] was too old for field service, or because she had so faithfully done the duties of her station in early life, I know not, but she enjoyed the special right of living in a cabin separate from the other cabins, having given her only the charge of the young children and the burden of her support. . . . The practice of separating mothers from their children and hiring them out at distances too great to allow their meeting, except after long periods of time, was a marked feature of the cruelty and hardness of the slave system. . . .

My grandmother's five daughters were hired out . . . and my only recollections of my own mother are of a few hasty visits made in the night on foot, after the daily tasks were over, and when she had to return in time to answer the driver's call to the field in the early morning. These little glimpses of my mother under such conditions and against such odds, meager as they were, are permanently stamped upon my memory. She was tall and had dark, glossy skin with regular features, and amongst the slaves was remarkably sedate and dignified.

DIRECTIONS: Use the passage above and other available resources to answer the following questions about Frederick Douglass on a separate sheet of paper. For each question, tell whether you used only the passage to find the answer or whether you needed to use an encyclopedia, a dictionary, or some other reference book.

1. When was Frederick Douglass born, and when did he die?
born: 1817; died: 1895; encyclopedia, dictionary, or some other reference book
2. In what state did Douglass live as a slave?
Maryland; encyclopedia, dictionary, or some other reference book
3. Who raised Douglass as a boy?
his grandparents; passage
4. How did Douglass describe his mother?
tall, with dark, glossy skin and regular features; sedate and dignified; passage

Harcourt Brace School Publishers

NAME _____ DATE _____

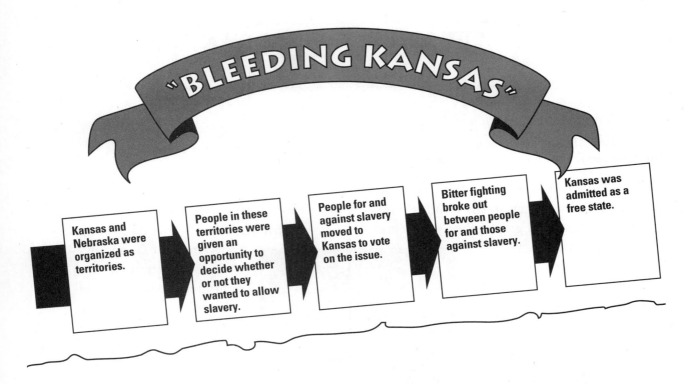

"BLEEDING KANSAS"

| Kansas and Nebraska were organized as territories. | People in these territories were given an opportunity to decide whether or not they wanted to allow slavery. | People for and against slavery moved to Kansas to vote on the issue. | Bitter fighting broke out between people for and those against slavery. | Kansas was admitted as a free state. |

Expand Thinking About an Issue

DIRECTIONS: Use the flow chart above and the information in your textbook to answer the questions below.

1. How did the Kansas–Nebraska Act deal with the spread of slavery?

   It allowed people in the Kansas and Nebraska territories to vote on whether or not they wanted slavery.

2. How do you think people in the North reacted to the Kansas–Nebraska Act?

   They probably opposed it because it could allow slavery in two more territories.

3. How do you think people in the South viewed the Kansas–Nebraska Act?

   They probably supported it because it could allow slavery in two more territories.

4. What were the major effects of the Kansas–Nebraska Act in Kansas?

   More people moved there; fighting broke out between those for and those against slavery.

5. Why did Southern states begin to talk more about secession after Kansas became a state?

   Because the North had more people, Southerners may possibly have come to believe they could not

   win future elections.

6. Do you think the Kansas–Nebraska Act was a good law? Why or why not?

   Accept any reasonable answer that students can defend.

Use after reading Chapter 13, Lesson 3, pages 490–495.

Harcourt Brace School Publishers

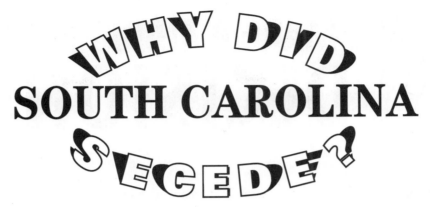

Recognize Point of View

DIRECTIONS: Read the following paragraph from the *South Carolina Secession Ordinance of December 20, 1860.*

SOUTH CAROLINA SECESSION ORDINANCE
December 20, 1860

An agreement between the states set up a government with specific purposes and powers. We feel that the reasons for which this government was begun have been defeated. The government itself has destroyed them by the action of the Northern, nonslaveholding states. **(1)** Those states have assumed the right to decide the properness of our domestic practices (that is, slavery). **(2)** They have denied our rights of property recognized by the Constitution. They have denounced as sinful the practice of slavery. **(3)** They have permitted the organization of abolitionist groups, whose goal is to disturb the peace of and to take away the property of the citizens of our states. **(4)** Those groups have encouraged and helped thousands of our slaves to leave their homes; and the slaves who remain have been incited by special agents, books, and pictures into insurrection.

DIRECTIONS: *For each numbered sentence in the South Carolina Secession Ordinance, state in your own words a South Carolina complaint from a Southern point of view. Then write a response that tells a Northern point of view. Use your textbook if you need more information.*

Southern Complaint   Northern Response

1. Northern states are trying to end slavery. _____

2. They are trying to take away property. _____ Accept any reasonable responses

3. They have allowed abolitionist groups. _____ that students can defend.

4. They encourage slaves to run away. _____

HOW TO MAKE A THOUGHTFUL DECISION

Apply Critical Thinking Skills

DIRECTIONS: Think about a decision you made recently at school, or think about a decision that someone made during the Civil War. Then use the organizer below to record and analyze that decision. Fill in as many possible actions and consequences as you can.

THE GOAL

Students' responses should demonstrate an ability to analyze decisions.

POSSIBLE ACTIONS	POSSIBLE CONSEQUENCES
1. _____	1. _____
2. _____	2. _____
3. _____	3. _____
4. _____	4. _____

THE CHOICE	REASONS FOR THE CHOICE

THE RESULT

Harcourt Brace School Publishers

Use after reading Chapter 13, Skill Lesson, page 501.

Background to the CONFLICT

Connect Main Ideas

DIRECTIONS: Use this organizer to show how the chapter's main ideas are connected. Write three details to support each main idea.

Differences Divide North and South
People in the North and the South disagreed during the mid-1800s.

1. The North had more people living in cities and more factories, while the South depended upon farming as a way of life.

2. As demand for cotton increased, Southern plantation owners used more slaves to help raise and harvest their crops.

3. Bad feelings over the growth of the North and the question of the spread of slavery to the frontier led to fierce arguments.

Africans in Slavery and Freedom
Enslaved people protested being held in slavery.

1. Some slaves secretly damaged the plantations they worked on.

2. Some slaves attacked people in rebellions. Some slaves used the Underground Railroad to reach freedom in the North.

3. _____

Background to the Conflict

Facing a National Problem
Northerners and Southerners tried to settle disagreements during the 1800s.

1. The Missouri Compromise balanced free and slave states and created an imaginary line between them. The Kansas-Nebraska Act

2. allowed people living in those territories to decide whether or not to allow slavery. The Compromise of 1850 allowed

3. people in New Mexico and Utah to decide whether or not to allow slavery and punished people who helped slaves escape.

A Time for Hard Decisions
Americans had to make important decisions in 1860 and 1861.

1. After Abraham Lincoln was elected President of the United States, South Carolina seceded from the Union.

2. Other states joined South Carolina to create the new country called the Confederate States of America.

3. After President Lincoln decided to send supply ships to Fort Sumter, Jefferson Davis decided to attack the fort— leading to the Civil War.

Harcourt Brace School Publishers

Use after reading Chapter 13, pages 476–505.

THE BONNIE BLUE FLAG

When South Carolina joined the Confederacy, its flag changed, but Harry Macarthy's song, "The Bonnie Blue Flag," which was about South Carolina's first flag, quickly became the Confederacy's national anthem.

Link Music to History

DIRECTIONS: Read the words to the song. Then answer the questions that follow.

Verse One
1. We are a band of brothers, and native to the soil,
2. Fighting for the property we gained by honest toil;
3. And when our rights were threatened, the cry rose near and far:
4. Hurrah! for the bonnie blue flag that bears a single star.

Verse Two
1. As long as the Union was faithful to her trust,
2. Like friends and like brothers, kind were we and just;
3. But now, when Northern treachery attempts our rights to mar,
4. We hoist, on high, the bonnie blue flag that bears a single star.

Last Verse
1. Then here's to our Confederacy—strong we are and brave,
2. Like patriots of old, we'll fight, our heritage to save;
3. And rather than submit to shame, to die we would prefer—
4. So cheer for the bonnie blue flag that bears a single star.

Chorus
1. Hurrah! hurrah! for Southern rights! hurrah!
2. Hurrah! for the bonnie blue flag that bears a single star.

1. Write the phrase that is repeated in line 4 of each verse.

bonnie blue flag, a single star
_____

2. Which line in Verse One describes how the Confederate soldiers felt about one another? Describe that feeling. Line 1; they felt as if they were brothers.
_____

3. Each verse has one line that states a reason that the Confederacy was fighting. List each line number and give the reason.

Verse One	Line Number: 2	Reason:	property
Verse Two	Line Number: 3	Reason:	rights
Last Verse	Line Number: 2	Reason:	heritage

Use after reading Chapter 14, Lesson 1, pages 507–513.

THE Emancipation Proclamation

Interpret Primary Source Documents

DIRECTIONS: *The passage below from the Emancipation Proclamation contains words in boldface type. Use context clues to define those words. Match each word in the list with its definition, and write the correct letter in the blank. Then, on a separate sheet of paper, answer the questions that follow.*

And by **virtue** of the power and for the purpose **aforesaid,** I do order and declare that all persons held as slaves within said **designated** States and parts of States are, and **henceforward** shall be, free; and that the Executive Government of the United States, including the military and naval authorities thereof, will recognize and maintain the freedom of said persons.

And I hereby enjoin upon the people so declared to be free to **abstain** from all violence, unless in necessary self-defense; and I recommend to them that, in all cases when allowed, they labor faithfully for reasonable wages.

And I further declare and make known that such persons of **suitable** condition will be received into the armed service of the United States to **garrison** forts, positions, stations, and other places, and to **man** vessels of all sorts in said service.

_C_ virtue	**A.** pointed out; shown	
_E_ aforesaid	**B.** from this time on	
_A_ designated	**C.** because of; on the grounds of	
_B_ henceforward	**D.** right; proper	
_H_ abstain	**E.** spoken of before; mentioned previously	
_D_ suitable	**F.** to station troops in a fort or town	
_F_ garrison	**G.** to take an assigned place for work or defense	
_G_ man	**H.** to keep oneself back; to choose not to do	

1. What is the most important message in the first paragraph?
the freeing of slaves in designated states

2. What did President Lincoln recommend to former slaves in the second paragraph?
that they not take part in violence and that they work for pay

3. In the last paragraph, what did President Lincoln declare about the armed services?
that the armed services would accept former slaves fit for duty for various positions

Harcourt Brace School Publishers

Use after reading Chapter 14, Lesson 2, pages 514–519.

★ CIVIL WAR ★
HORSES

Apply Information from a Chart

DIRECTIONS: Study the chart below. Then complete the activities that follow.

CIVIL WAR GENERALS' HORSES

HORSE'S NAME	RIDER'S NAME	ARMY	DESCRIPTION	FURTHERMORE
Don Juan	George Armstrong Custer ★	Union	Bay stallion	Custer had more horses (7) killed under him than any other Union leader.
Butler	Wade Hampton ★	Confederate	Bay stallion	One of Hampton's officers gave him the horse as a gift.
Sam	William Tecumseh Sherman ★	Union	Half-breed bay stallion	The horse was so steady under gunfire that Sherman could write orders while riding.
Lexington	William Tecumseh Sherman	Union	Kentucky thoroughbred	Sherman rode Lexington during his final review of his army.
Traveller	Robert E. Lee	Confederate	Iron gray gelding	Traveller was called the greatest warhorse of all time, except for Alexander the Great's horse.
Old Spot	Judson Kilpatrick	Union	Arabian	The horse outlived his master.

1. Underline the name of the general who had seven horses killed under him.

2. Put a star next to the name of each general who rode a bay stallion.

3. Put a box around the name of the horse that outlived his master.

4. a) Imagine you are a Civil War general. Explain why it is important to choose a good horse.

Accept all reasonable answers that show an understanding of the role horses played in battle.

_____

_____

b) Which of the horses on the chart would you have chosen? Explain your answer.

Answers should substantiate the choice, using information in the chart.

_____

_____

Use after reading Chapter 14, Lesson 3, pages 520–527.

Harcourt Brace School Publishers

NAME _____ DATE _____

HOW TO COMPARE MAPS with DIFFERENT SCALES

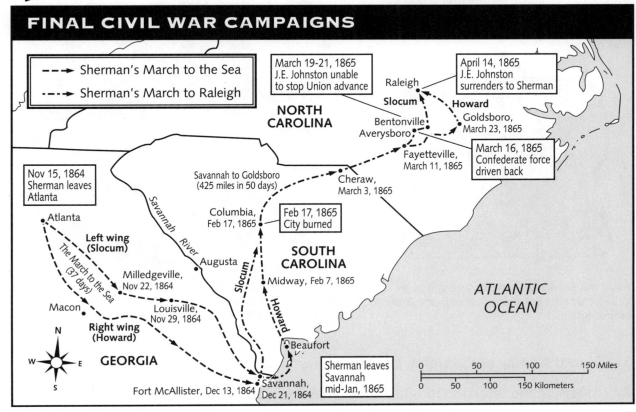

FINAL CIVIL WAR CAMPAIGNS

- - → Sherman's March to the Sea
- · → Sherman's March to Raleigh

March 19-21, 1865
J.E. Johnston unable
to stop Union advance

April 14, 1865
J.E. Johnston
surrenders to Sherman

Raleigh

Slocum   **Howard**

**NORTH
CAROLINA**

Bentonville
Averysboro

Goldsboro,
March 23, 1865

March 16, 1865
Confederate force
driven back

Fayetteville,
March 11, 1865

Nov 15, 1864
Sherman leaves
Atlanta

Savannah to Goldsboro
(425 miles in 50 days)

Cheraw,
March 3, 1865

Atlanta

Columbia,
Feb 17, 1865

Feb 17, 1865
City burned

**Left wing
(Slocum)**

Savannah River

**SOUTH
CAROLINA**

Augusta

The March to the Sea
(37 days)

Milledgeville,
Nov 22, 1864

Slocum

Midway, Feb 7, 1865

**ATLANTIC
OCEAN**

Macon

Louisville,
Nov 29, 1864

Howard

**Right wing
(Howard)**

N
W E
S

GEORGIA

Beaufort

Fort McAllister, Dec 13, 1864

Savannah,
Dec 21, 1864

Sherman leaves
Savannah
mid-Jan, 1865

| 0 | 50 | 100 | 150 Miles |
| 0 | 50 | 100 | 150 Kilometers |

Apply Map and Globe Skills

**DIRECTIONS: Compare the map above with the map in your textbook on page 525.
For each of the following statements, decide which map is more useful. Write A in the
answer blank if the map above is better and B if the textbook map is better.**

_____B_____ **1.** Show the most miles per inch.

_____A_____ **2.** Determine the distance between Cheraw and Fayetteville.

_____A_____ **3.** Determine how many miles Sherman traveled on his March to the Sea.

_____B_____ **4.** Identify the extent of the Union blockade.

_____A_____ **5.** Measure the distance from Atlanta, Georgia, to Macon, Georgia.

_____B_____ **6.** Identify battles that took place in Mississippi and Virginia.

_____A_____ **7.** Determine the number of miles traveled by Sherman's army between February 17, 1865, and March 11, 1865.

Use after reading Chapter 14, Skill Lesson, pages 528–529.

ACTIVITY BOOK 95

IT'S IN THE BAG!

Interpret Visuals and Point of View

DIRECTIONS: Study the illustrations and the captions below. Then on a separate sheet of paper, answer the questions that follow.

After the Civil War inexpensive suitcases called carpetbags (above) were made from carpeting.

THE MAN WITH THE (CARPET) BAGS
Cartoonist Thomas Nast helped shape the U.S. public's view of Reconstruction. This 1872 cartoon shows a former Union general.

1. Circle the name of the Union general in Nast's cartoon.

2. Underline the direction in which the general is heading.

3. Compare the bags in the cartoon with the one in the illustration next to the cartoon. What similarities and differences do you notice? Answers should describe similarities and differences in shape, size, texture, handle, design, and so on.

4. Look at the illustration on the left. How do you think this type of bag got its name? It was made out of carpeting.

5. How do you think Nast viewed the type of person in this cartoon? List the features of this cartoon that support your answer. Nast probably did not think highly of the carpetbaggers. Accept any features of the cartoon that students can support.

6. Nast said about this cartoon, "The bag in front of him, filled with others' faults, he always sees. The one behind him, filled with his own faults, he never sees." Explain what you think Nast meant. Answers should point out that the character is trying to fix someone else's faults (the South's) without fixing his own (the North's) first.

Use after reading Chapter 14, Lesson 4, pages 530–537.

Civil War and Reconstruction

Connect Main Ideas

DIRECTIONS: Use this organizer to show how the chapter's main ideas are connected. Write a sentence or two telling how each event or idea affected the lives of Americans during the Civil War and Reconstruction.

Choosing Sides
Most Northerners supported the Union, wanting to help maintain the government. Most Southerners supported the Confederacy, wanting to win their independence. Others had a difficult choice to make, especially those people who lived in border states or Indian nations.

Emancipation Proclamation
President Lincoln signed an order to free slaves in states that had seceded.

Civil War and Reconstruction

Union Victories
Union victories such as the battles of Vicksburg and Gettysburg as well as General Sherman's March to the Sea forced General Lee to surrender his ragged troops in April 1865.

Rebuilding America
President Johnson pardoned most Confederates who promised loyalty to the United States and said that the Confederate states must abolish slavery.

Congress wanted a plan that was tougher on white Southerners than President Johnson's plan.

Use after reading Chapter 14, pages 506–539.

Famous Entrepreneurs

Categorize Information

DIRECTIONS: Read the stories that follow, and use the information to fill in the chart. Use your textbook and library reference materials to fill in the information about Andrew Carnegie.

Levi Strauss, a Jewish immigrant from Germany, left New York City for the West in 1850. He went west to sell canvas to settlers to use for sails and coverings for their wagons. When he arrived there, he found that settlers could not find pants strong enough to last. Strauss took his canvas material and made it into the first pair of jeans. His company became Levi Strauss & Co.

John Harvey Kellogg, of British ancestry, believed that a healthful diet would help people heal more quickly from illness. He was once sued by an elderly woman who broke her false teeth on a zwieback (hard bread) that he had recommended for her to eat. As a result of this incident, he started to think about producing a softer ready-to-eat food. One night he dreamed of how to make flaked foods. This dream resulted in his producing the first dry cereal, which today is known as Kellogg's Cornflakes.

Fannie Merritt Farmer was born in Boston of British descent. She suffered a childhood illness that left her with a limp. After doctors discouraged her from going to college, she entered cooking school in 1887. By 1891 she was running it! In those days, cooking ingredients were measured by "pinches and dabs." Farmer applied science to cooking. In her best-selling cookbook, she standardized measurements. You can thank her for the level teaspoon.

FAMOUS ENTREPRENEURS			
ENTREPRENEUR	**HERITAGE**	**COMPANY/PRODUCT**	**FUN FACT**
Levi Strauss	German	Levi Strauss & Co./ jeans	Accept all answers students can verify.
John Harvey Kellogg	British	Kellogg's/cereals	
Fannie Merritt Farmer	British	cooking school; cookbook/food	
Andrew Carnegie	Scottish	Carnegie Steel/ steel	

Harcourt Brace School Publishers

Use after reading Chapter 15, Lesson 1, pages 555–559.

HOW TO USE A Time Zone MAP

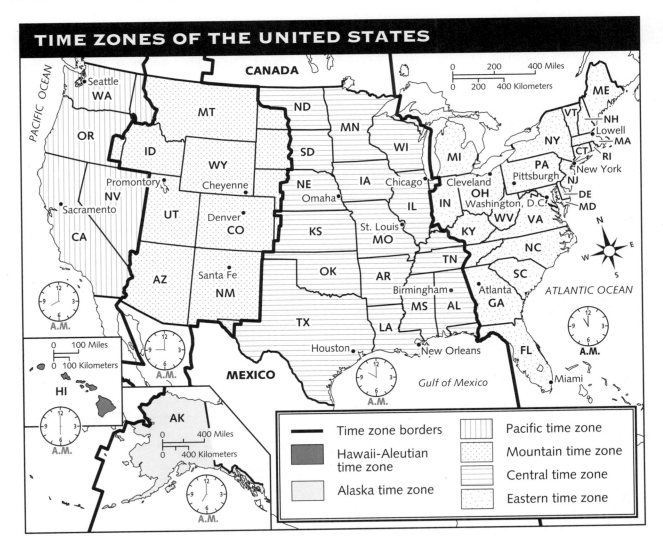

Apply Map and Globe Skills

DIRECTIONS: Study the time zone map below. The clock in the eastern time zone is set at 11:00 A.M. Draw the hands on the clocks in the other time zones, and note whether the time shown is A.M. or P.M. Then use different colors to shade in the time zones on the map and the key.

TIME ZONES OF THE UNITED STATES

CANADA

200   400 Miles
200   400 Kilometers

Seattle
WA
MT
ND
MN
ME
VT
NH
Lowell
MA
NY
CT
RI
New York
PA
Pittsburgh
NJ
DE
MD

OR
ID
WY
Cheyenne
SD
WI
MI
Promontory
NV
Sacramento
UT
Denver
CO
NE
Omaha
IA
Chicago
IL
IN
Cleveland
OH
Washington, D.C.
WV
VA
KY

CA
AZ
Santa Fe
NM
KS
St. Louis
MO
NC
TN
SC

OK
AR
Birmingham
MS
AL
Atlanta
GA
ATLANTIC OCEAN

TX
LA
Houston
New Orleans
FL
Miami

A.M.

A.M.

A.M.

A.M.

100 Miles
100 Kilometers
HI

MEXICO

Gulf of Mexico

AK
400 Miles
400 Kilometers

A.M.

A.M.

Time zone borders	Pacific time zone
Hawaii-Aleutian time zone	Mountain time zone
Alaska time zone	Central time zone
	Eastern time zone

(continued)

NAME _____ DATE _____

DIRECTIONS: Study the time zone map on page 99. Complete the activities that follow.

1. How many time zones are located in the United States? 6 _____

2. In which time zone is your city located? Answers should state appropriate time zone. _____

3. In which time zones are the following cities located:

Chicago, Illinois central _____   St. Louis, Missouri central _____

Cleveland, Ohio eastern _____   Atlanta, Georgia eastern _____

4. Andrew Carnegie produced his steel in Pittsburgh, Pennsylvania. If he transported it by railroad from Pittsburgh to the West Coast, through how many time zones would the steel travel? 4 _____

5. John D. Rockefeller set up an oil refinery in Cleveland, Ohio. He later bought refineries in West Virginia. If he traveled from his refinery in Ohio to his refinery in West Virginia, through how many time zones would he travel? One; both states are in the same time zone. _____

6. The Union Pacific Railroad built west from Omaha, Nebraska. The Central Pacific Railroad built east from Sacramento, California.

A. If it is 7:00 P.M. in Sacramento, what time is it in Omaha? 9:00 P.M. _____

B. If it is 8:00 A.M. in Omaha, what time is it in Sacramento? 6:00 A.M. _____

7. The two railroads met at Promontory, Utah. If it is 10 A.M. in Promontory,

A. What time is it in Omaha? 11:00 A.M. _____

B. What time is it in Sacramento? 9:00 A.M. _____

8. If the Super Bowl aired on TV from New Orleans at 3:00 P.M., what time would sports fans in Hawaii have to turn on their television sets to see the game? 11:00 A.M. _____

9. Imagine you live in Denver, Colorado, and have a scheduled school lunch at noon.

A. What time would it be in our nation's capital? 2:00 P.M. _____

B. What do you think students in the nation's capital would be doing at that time?
Accept all answers that students can support, such as attending their last class or getting ready to go home from school.

Use after reading Chapter 15, Skill Lesson, pages 560–561.

Harcourt Brace School Publishers

Duke Ellington

Interpret Information

DIRECTIONS: Read the paragraph below about one of the world's greatest jazz musicians, Duke Ellington. Then answer the questions that follow.

Duke Ellington was born in 1899 in Washington, D.C. He wrote music, led bands, and played the piano. In the 1920s he moved to Harlem, in New York City, to be a part of the large and growing African American community of artists and musicians living there. His band played in concert halls and theaters all over the world. Duke Ellington wrote more than 1,500 songs, including music for Broadway plays and motion pictures. Much of his music is now part of the Duke Ellington Collection at the Smithsonian Institution in Washington, D.C.

1. Why did Duke Ellington want to move to Harlem?

Accept answers that say he wanted to be a part of the community of African American

artists and musicians living there.

2. How did inventions like the phonograph and the radio help Duke Ellington and his band become known by many people?

Responses should state that many people had access to record albums, phonographs, and radios,

which allowed Duke Ellington's music to be heard by many people.

3. Duke Ellington wrote music for plays and motion pictures. What changes in American life do you think gave people more time to enjoy plays and motion pictures?

Accept answers that reflect the fact that advances in industry and transportation helped people get work

done faster, which helped them have more free time to enjoy their lives.

4. Why do you think it's important that much of Duke Ellington's music is part of the Duke Ellington Collection at the Smithsonian Institution in Washington, D.C.?

Possible responses could include the fact that at the Smithsonian Duke Ellington's music will be kept as

historical documents. Our musical heritage is important because it tells us about our past.

ORGANIZING
Resources

Understand Economics

DIRECTIONS: Three kinds of resources are needed to make a product: natural resources, or raw materials, such as minerals and ores; capital resources, such as money, tools, and equipment; and human resources, or workers. Conduct library research and complete the organizer below to show what resources are needed to make each product listed in the center box.

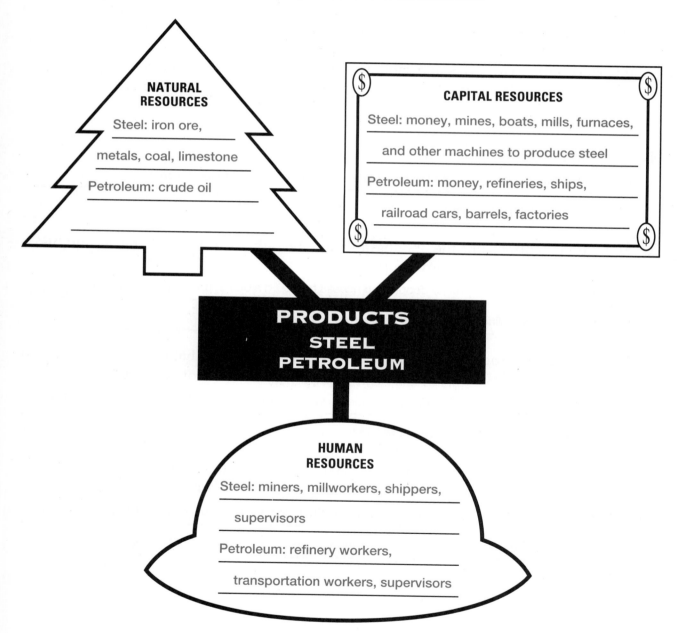

NATURAL RESOURCES

Steel: iron ore,

metals, coal, limestone

Petroleum: crude oil

_____

CAPITAL RESOURCES

Steel: money, mines, boats, mills, furnaces,

and other machines to produce steel

Petroleum: money, refineries, ships,

railroad cars, barrels, factories

PRODUCTS
STEEL
PETROLEUM

HUMAN RESOURCES

Steel: miners, millworkers, shippers,

supervisors

Petroleum: refinery workers,

transportation workers, supervisors

Harcourt Brace School Publishers

School Days

Relate Past to Present

DIRECTIONS: **The following excerpt from** Immigrant Kids **by Russell Freedman describes a typical school day in New York City in the early 1900s. Read the excerpt. Then answer the questions that follow.**

When teacher called out in her sharp, penetrating voice, "Class!" everyone sat up straight as a ramrod, eyes front, hands clasped rigidly behind one's back. We strived painfully to please her. With a thin smile of approval on her face, her eyes roved over the stiff, rigid figures in front of her.

Beautiful script letters across the huge blackboard and a chart of the alphabet were the sole adornments of the classroom. Every day the current lesson from our speller was meticulously written out on the blackboard by the teacher. . . . We spent hours over our copybooks, all conveniently lined, as we laboriously sought to imitate this perfection.

We had to learn our lessons by heart, and we repeated them out loud until we memorized them. Playgrounds were nonexistent, toilets were in the yard, and gymnasiums were an unheard-of luxury.

1. Use context clues to define *penetrating*. <u>Possible answers include "sharp," "piercing," and "deep."</u>

2. Use context clues to describe your image of a ramrod. <u>Accept all answers that describe</u>

<u>something rigid or unyielding. Discuss with students the definition of *ramrod*: "a rod used for</u>

<u>ramming down the charge in a gun that is loaded through the muzzle."</u>

3. Compare the adornments, or decorations, in the classroom described with the ones in your classroom. <u>Responses should describe both differences and similarities.</u>

_____

4. Describe differences between the way the teacher presented lessons in the early 1900s and the way your teacher presents lessons. Include descriptions of methods and materials. <u>Responses should address the use of the blackboard, copybooks, and memorization compared</u>

<u>with computers, textbooks, and examples of higher-order thinking skills.</u>

5. On a separate sheet of paper, write three paragraphs about your school, using the above three paragraphs as a guide. Describe the same things described in each paragraph, but use your school and class as the topic. Responses should parallel description provided in each paragraph.

Harcourt Brace School Publishers

HOW TO SOLVE A PROBLEM

Apply Critical Thinking Skills

DIRECTIONS: *Choose a problem in your school, such as one related to school lunches, bus schedules, or class size. Use the flow chart below to suggest a solution. You may copy the flow chart onto a separate sheet of paper if necessary.* Responses should address a specific school problem.

Decide what the problem is. List the problem.

_____

_____

Think of possible solutions. List the solutions.

_____

_____

Think about the possible results of each solution. List the possible results of each solution.

_____

_____

Choose one solution. List this solution.

_____

_____

Think about how well your solution solves the problem. Explain how your solution solves the problem.

_____

_____

Use after reading Chapter 15, Skill Lesson, page 579.

Harcourt Brace School Publishers

A Changing America

Connect Main Ideas

DIRECTIONS: Use this organizer to show how the chapter's main ideas are connected. Complete the organizer by writing two or three sentences that summarize the main idea of each lesson.

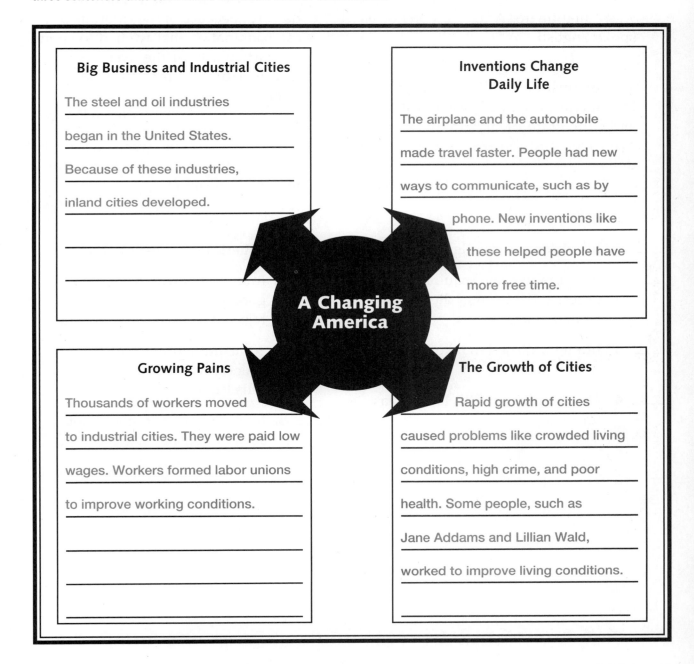

Big Business and Industrial Cities

The steel and oil industries

began in the United States.

Because of these industries,

inland cities developed.

Inventions Change Daily Life

The airplane and the automobile

made travel faster. People had new

ways to communicate, such as by

phone. New inventions like

these helped people have

more free time.

A Changing America

Growing Pains

Thousands of workers moved

to industrial cities. They were paid low

wages. Workers formed labor unions

to improve working conditions.

The Growth of Cities

Rapid growth of cities

caused problems like crowded living

conditions, high crime, and poor

health. Some people, such as

Jane Addams and Lillian Wald,

worked to improve living conditions.

Immigration

Distinguish Fact from Opinion

DIRECTIONS: Study the quotations below, which were made by immigrants who came to the United States at the beginning of the twentieth century. Then decide which of the following statements is fact and which is opinion. Write an F next to the statements of fact. Write an O next to the statements of opinion.

As far as Ellis Island was concerned, it was a nightmare. After all, none of us spoke English.

Nina Goodenov

The examiner [at Ellis Island] sat bureaucratically . . . I was questioned as to the state of my finances and I produced the required twenty-five dollars.

Louis Adamic

We lived there [Ellis Island] for three days . . . Because of the rigorous physical examination that we had to submit to, particularly of the eyes, there was this terrible anxiety that one of us might be rejected.

Angelo Pellegrini

America is . . . the great Melting Pot where all the races of Europe are melting and re-forming.

Israel Zangwill

O **1.** Ellis Island was a nightmare.

F **2.** Immigrants were required to produce $25 to enter the United States.

F **3.** Immigrants had to take a physical examination.

O **4.** The examiner at Ellis Island was unfriendly.

O **5.** America is a great Melting Pot.

F **6.** Immigrants who were not in good physical health could be rejected from the United States.

F **7.** Some immigrants had to spend several days waiting on Ellis Island.

F **8.** Many immigrants could not speak English.

   Use after reading Chapter 16, Lesson 1, pages 583–589.

HOW TO COMPARE Information on Graphs

Apply Chart and Graph Skills

DIRECTIONS: Use the information in the bar graph and the circle graph below to answer the questions that follow.

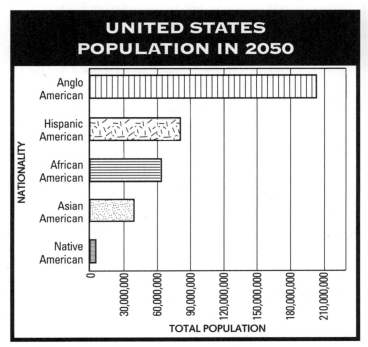

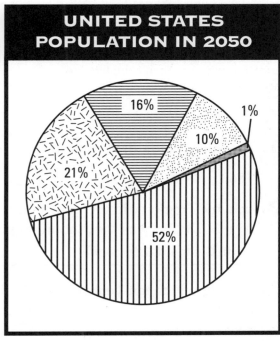

1. Which graph would you use to find the total number of Asian Americans living in the United States in 2050? __the bar graph_____

2. What will be the percentage of Asian Americans and African Americans in the United States in 2050? __16% + 10% = 26%_____ Which graph did you use to find the percentage of Asian Americans and African Americans? __the circle graph_____

3. Which nationality will make up the second-largest percentage of the population in 2050? __Hispanic American_____

4. Which nationality will have a population of about 40,000,000 in 2050? __Asian American___

5. What will be the percentage of Native Americans in the United States in 2050? __1%____

   Does this percentage represent more than or less than 30,000,000 people? __less than____

AN African American PORTRAIT

Read a Table

DIRECTIONS: *Study this table, which shows what percentage of the African American population lived in different regions of the United States during different time periods. Look for patterns. Then complete the activities that follow.*

AFRICAN AMERICANS IN THE UNITED STATES, BY REGION (in percentages)

YEAR	NORTHEAST	NORTH CENTRAL	SOUTH	WEST
1860	3.5	4.1	92.2	0.1
1870	3.7	5.6	90.6	0.1
1880	3.5	5.9	90.5	0.2
1890	3.6	5.8	90.3	0.4
1900	4.4	5.6	89.7	0.3
1910	4.9	5.5	89.0	0.5
1920	6.5	7.6	85.2	0.8
1930	9.6	10.6	78.7	1.0

1. In which region did the percentage of African Americans decrease steadily from

1860 to 1930? South _____

2. In which region did the percentage of African Americans increase the most from 1860 to 1930? What was the amount of percentage increase in this region?

North Central; 6.5 percent

_____

3. During which ten-year period did the percentage of African Americans living in the South decrease the most? How much of a decrease was there during this period?

1920 to 1930; 6.5 percent

_____

4. Migration was one reason that the percentage of African Americans in the South decreased during this time. Reread Jacob Lawrence's *The Great Migration: An American Story* in your textbook. Look for reasons that African Americans migrated. Copy the following headings onto a separate sheet of paper, and use information from the story to complete a chart showing reasons for African American migration.

FACTORS PUSHING AFRICAN AMERICANS OUT OF THE SOUTH	FACTORS PULLING AFRICAN AMERICANS TO OTHER REGIONS
floods ruined farms, boll weevil destroyed cotton crops, high cost of food, lack of justice in courts, harsh and unfair treatment by white landowners, segregation, limited opportunity for education	need for factory workers, workers were lent money to purchase railroad tickets, promise of better housing, letters from relatives living in the North

Harcourt Brace School Publishers

Sing About CIVIL RIGHTS

Link Music to History

DIRECTIONS: Read the words to the following civil rights song "If You Miss Me from the Back of the Bus." Then answer the questions and complete the activities that follow.

If you miss me from the back of the bus,
And you can't find me nowhere,
Come on up to the front of the bus,
I'll be riding up there,
I'll be riding up there,
I'll be riding up there.
Come on up to the front of the bus,
I'll be riding up there.

If you miss me from the front of the bus,
And you can't find me nowhere,
Come on up to the driver's seat,
I'll be drivin' up there.
I'll be drivin' up there,
I'll be drivin' up there,
Come on up to the driver's seat,
I'll be drivin' up there.

1. Who does "me" represent in the song? African Americans
_____

2. Circle the words that describe the part of the bus where members of this group were

<u>first</u> required to sit. Why did they sit there? Segregation laws required them to do so.
_____

_____

3. In the second verse of the song, who is in the driver's seat?
an African American
_____

4. What is the purpose of this protest song? Answers should include references to nonviolent
_____
means of achieving equal rights.

_____

5. Describe in your own words what civil rights mean to you. Accept answers that reflect an
_____
understanding of equal rights and the rights guaranteed by Amendments 13, 14, 15, and 19 of the

U.S. Constitution.
_____

_____

HOW TO ACT AS A RESPONSIBLE CITIZEN

Citizens of the United States have certain rights that are guaranteed by the Constitution. However, people have to help protect these rights by being responsible citizens.

Apply Participation Skills

DIRECTIONS: Several rights of United States citizens are listed below. For each right, write two ways that people can be responsible citizens and protect their rights.

These responsibilities are possible responses.

Right: Freedom of speech

    Responsibility 1: Make sure what you say does not harm other people.

    Responsibility 2: Know what is happening in the community.

Right: Freedom to gather in groups

    Responsibility 1: Obey laws about gathering in groups.

    Responsibility 2: Gather peaceably with others.

Right: Voting

    Responsibility 1: Stay informed about issues of leadership and laws.

    Responsibility 2: On election day, vote to decide laws and choose leaders.

Right: Being a member of a jury trial

    Responsibility 1: Serve as a jury member.

    Responsibility 2: Follow the court's rules during a jury trial.

Right: Holding public office

    Responsibility 1: Staying well informed about current events.

    Responsibility 2: Respect the beliefs and ideas of others.

Harcourt Brace School Publishers

Use after reading Chapter 16, Skill Lesson, page 606.

An American Song

A song that tells of the beauty of America is "My Country 'Tis of Thee." The words to the song were written in 1831 by the Reverend Samuel F. Smith. Read the first two verses of the song.

My country, 'tis of thee,
Sweet Land of Liberty,
  Of thee I sing;
Land where my fathers died,
Land of the pilgrims' pride,
From every mountain side
  Let Freedom ring.

My native country, thee,
Land of the noble free, —
  Thy name I love;
I love thy rocks and rills,
Thy woods and templed hills,
My heart with rapture thrills
  Like that above.

Identify and Interpret Patriotic Songs

DIRECTIONS: Below are some lines from the song. For each line, write what you think the words mean or draw a picture that illustrates the meaning of the words.

1. "Sweet Land of Liberty,"

Accept all responses that link a logical patriotic image or theme to the words. Students should be able to defend their answers.

2. "Land of the pilgrims' pride,"

3. "I love thy rocks and rills [brooks],"

4. "Thy woods and templed hills,"

Use after reading Chapter 16, Lesson 4, pages 607–609.

The Promise of America

Connect Main Ideas

DIRECTIONS: Use this organizer to show how the chapter's main ideas are connected. Write three details to support each main idea.

Immigrants in the United States faced problems.

1. Immigrants faced prejudice from people born in the United States.

2. Immigrants earned very low wages.

3. Immigrant families lived together in crowded, dirty tenements.

African Americans shared problems with other newcomers to cities.

1. Families lived in crowded, dirty quarters.

2. Northerners did not welcome migrants because they had to compete with them for housing and jobs.

3. Migrants experienced segregation.

The Promise of America

Individuals worked to improve life in the United States in the twentieth century.

1. Booker T. Washington and W.E.B. DuBois worked to solve problems of economic hardships.

2. Martin Luther King, Jr., received Nobel Peace Prize for his use of nonviolent ways to bring about change.

3. Betty Friedan and others started NOW to work to ensure that women have equal job opportunities.

Citizens of the United States contribute to their communities and our nation as a whole.

1. Vote to choose leaders and decide laws.

2. Be aware of current events.

3. Volunteer to help the community.

Use after reading Chapter 16, pages 582–611.